HOU~~DINI~~

About Higher Read™

Take learning out of the ivory tower and into your hands. With Higher Read's™ original content, you have all the expertise of professionals in a convenient, accessible format. From organizing to learning about history to writing like a pro, continue your education with Higher Read's™ real-life guides and how-tos. Because doctors, lawyers, writers, and college professors contribute to the curriculum, you will read it and then you will know it.

We'd love to hear from you. If you have questions, comments, complaints, or compliments, please contact us at info@HigherRead.com or visit us online at www.HigherRead.com

Foreword

From the Publisher

Houdini was a man of magic and mystery. He was also a pilot, an author, an actor, and a rabid opponent of the Spiritualist movement. He was impatient of charlatans and imitators and loving to his family. He had an impressive ego. If any of these facts are new to you, then *Houdini: A Life Worth Reading* is the perfect primer on the man who was, by the end of his life, known only as Houdini.

From his Nude Cell Escape (yes, that is exactly like it sounds) to his methodical debunking of mediums, Houdini orchestrated his talent, persona, and career with care, enthusiasm, and determination.

With an easy-to-read biography, writings from Houdini himself, and quick-fact introductions to each chapter, *Houdini: A Life Worth Reading* will tell you what you want most to know about the King of Handcuffs, also known as Ehrich Weisz, also known as the great Houdini.

Table of Contents

How This Book Is Organized

What You Will Find in Every Part

"Read It and Know It" sections appear at the beginning of each chapter. These features include brief facts to help you remember important details about the life of Houdini. Use this knowledge at cocktail parties or when you finally land that spot on Jeopardy.

"Know More About" sections appear throughout the text. These are quick and simple summaries of key concepts. Get to know these and you'll be sure to impress your friends or that know-it-all at work. You can read the book from front to end or you can skip to areas you think sound interesting; there's no wrong way to read this book.

"In Houdini's Words" also appear throughout the text. These sections take Houdini's words as he wrote them and put them in context for you. By reading Houdini's words alongside his biography, you will increase your understanding of these primary sources.

"Test Your Knowledge" sections appear at the end of the book. These questions test you on key ideas for each chapter and help you remember main points. Use the Answer Key to check your knowledge. Take the quizzes right after reading the chapter or at the end of the book to discover what you remember of Houdini's life and times.

Introduction: Houdini, The Legend

The name Houdini is synonymous with intrigue, magic, and delight. In the history of magic, many performers have amazed, but only Houdini seems to have become the legend that symbolizes the very essence of what it means to be mystified and enthralled.

Magicians notoriously guard their secrets carefully, revealing them to very few outside of the trade, and Houdini was no exception. Some of those secrets he took to his grave. Many of Houdini's tricks and illusions are still sought after by young and experienced magicians alike.

But Houdini was much more than a mere stage presence; he was a driven, dedicated, death-defying artist who changed the field of magic forever. His many faces, including that of writer, actor, movie producer, collector of literature, and aviator, reveal a man who refused to accept any limits on his capacity to learn, evolve, and amaze.

I. Ehrich Weiss, the Child who Became Houdini

Read It and Know It

After reading this chapter, you will know more about

- **Houdini's birth:** The famous magician was born in Hungary on March 24, 1874.
- **Houdini's father:** Mayer Samuel Weisz was a rabbi and passed his love of learning on to his son.
- **The early years:** The Weisz family was poor, and their later-famous son ran away to ease their financial burden.
- **An early interest in performing:** In addition to performing for his family as early as nine years old, Houdini learned about magic from his friend Jacob Hyman.

The man who later became known as Houdini was born on March 24, 1874 in Budapest, Hungary. The name given to him at birth was Ehrich Weisz. Ehrich was the third child born to Rabbi Mayer Samuel Weisz and Cecilia Steiner.

Mayer Weisz was a rabbi with several advanced degrees. A scholar and poet, he practiced German Reform Judaism and spoke German and Hebrew in addition to his native language, Hungarian. Mayer had been married once before he married Ehrich's mother and had a fourteen-year-old son named Herman at the time of his marriage to Cecilia.

Cecilia Steiner was twelve years younger than her husband. She and Mayer had five boys and one girl together: Nathan, William, Ehrich, Theodore, Leopold, and Gladys, each between two and three years apart in age.

When Mayer was forty-seven years old, he came on his own to the United States, seeking a better life for his family. He changed the spelling of his name from Weisz to Weiss. Despite his inability to speak English, Mayer found a job as a rabbi in Appleton, Wisconsin, which had a small Jewish community. After two years, he saved enough money to send for his wife and four young children, including Ehrich. While the position in Appleton had seemed promising, Mayer made very little money at this job. Soon the congregation wanted a rabbi who was more modern and who spoke English. Mayer was fired after only four years. During that time, two more children were born to the family.

Desperate to make a living for his family, Mayer moved the Weisses to Milwaukee, which had a growing Jewish population due to the arrival of families fleeing anti-Semitic violence in Russia. However, the Jewish families in Milwaukee did not practice a strict form of Judaism, and there was no demand for Mayer's services as a rabbi. Mayer tried to earn money by conducting private religious services and by opening a school, but was unable to provide for his family. The poverty-stricken Weisses moved from one address to another, and Ehrich worked at odd jobs such as shoe-shining and selling newspapers to make money to support the family.

Ehrich's older half-brother Herman did not live long after the move to Milwaukee. He married (a woman who was not Jewish), and Mayer sent Herman to New York City to get him away from what he felt were bad influences in Milwaukee. Herman died there of tuberculosis at the age of twenty-two.

First Escape and Establishment in New York City

Ehrich ran away from home at the age of twelve, hoping to spare his parents the expense of providing for him and planning to earn money to send home. He left home without a change of clothes or food, and took a train that he believed was headed to Galveston, Texas. The train was actually bound for Kansas City, Missouri. When Ehrich arrived, he followed a rural road to a town called Delavan on the Wisconsin border. A kindly middle-aged couple, the Flitcrofts, gave Ehrich a place to live while he earned a living shining shoes and selling newspapers on the streets. Ehrich was able to send a small amount of money home. Ehrich always remembered Mrs. Flitcroft and gave her expensive gifts later on in his life.

While living in Delavan, Ehrich learned that his father had gone to New York City to seek a better fortune, temporarily leaving his family behind in Milwaukee. Ehrich traveled to New York City to join his father sometime in 1887, when he was merely thirteen years old. He and Mayer lived in a boarding house in the city until the rest of the family came to New York the following year. The family moved into an apartment in a four-story tenement house.

Mayer tried to earn money as a Hebrew teacher and by performing rabbinical services, but was again unable to make a living wage. Mayer sold his collection of Hebrew books to a local rabbi, and some accounts indicate he went to work at a clothing factory. Ehrich also worked at the clothing factory, as well as at various other jobs, including as a messenger-boy for large companies and at a tool-and-die shop. Even though he was technically enrolled at a local Jewish school, Ehrich did not have very much time to attend classes, and the son of educated Rabbi Weiss grew up with little formal education. Later in life, Houdini worked hard to establish himself as an educated man through his literary forays and many efforts to engage with academics.

Mayer Weiss died in New York City in 1892 following complications from surgery performed to treat tongue cancer. Houdini later reported that as Mayer lay dying, he made Ehrich promise to provide for his mother for the rest of her life.

Origins of Interest in Magic

When Ehrich was very young, he saw a trapeze artist in Appleton, Wisconsin and became obsessed. At the age of nine, Ehrich put on red stockings and performed his own trapeze act in his backyard, charging five cents and calling himself Eric, Prince of the Air. In this act, he hung from a trapeze and picked up pins from the ground with his teeth.

Ehrich was obsessed with physical abilities and taught himself how to do acrobatics and contortionist stunts. As a teenager in New York City, Ehrich became an avid runner and joined the Pastime Athletic Club. He reportedly trained by running ten miles a day in Central Park. He won a race organized by the Amateur Athletic Union even though he was not technically old enough to have entered. A famous picture of young Houdini shows him in his running uniform, his top covered with medals, some of them actually earned, and some of them put there by Ehrich for show. At seventeen, Ehrich was already as tall as he would ever become, only five feet four inches, with a muscular, stocky build.

Ehrich met his friend Jacob Hyman while working at the clothing factory in New York. Jacob was a young coworker and also an amateur magician, and he began to show Ehrich some of his tricks. Around that time, Ehrich bought a cheap copy of the biography of the famous French magician Jean-Eugène Robert-Houdin. According to Houdini's later writings, Ehrich was fascinated with Robert-Houdin, whom he then regarded as his hero.

Know More About: Houdini's Names

Although he eventually settled on "Houdini" alone, the King of Handcuffs had a plethora of names, not just a stage name and a birth name.

As a young child he was Ehrich Weisz. There are other spellings of this name: Erich Weisz and Erik Weiss. Erik is the name on his Hungarian birth certificate, but the name he and his family used while he was growing up was Ehrich.

When he moved to America his last name, and the name of his entire family, became Weiss. His nickname amongst friends and family was Ehrie. Ehrie then changed to Harry when he became Harry Houdini. Later he dropped the "Harry" and became Houdini.

He wasn't just Houdini on stage, either. Houdini's name changes were often all encompassing, and friends and family had to adapt to the different names in his personal life as well as his professional one.

In Houdini's Words

In *The Unmasking of Robert-Houdin*, Houdini remembers his early love of Robert-Houdin and describes it to the reader.

When it became necessary for me to take a stage-name, and a fellow-player, possessing a veneer of culture, told me that if I would add the letter "i" to Houdin's name, it would mean, in the French language, "like Houdin," I adopted the suggestion with enthusiasm. I asked nothing more of life than to become in my profession "like Robert-Houdin."

II. Houdini, the Struggling Magician

Read It and Know It

After reading this chapter, you will know more about

- **The Brothers Houdini:** Houdini and his friend Jacob Hyman performed together in an early magic act with this name, although more than one person would partner with Houdini in the act.
- **Houdini's early tricks:** "Metamorphosis" was an early escape trick of the type that would later make Houdini famous.
- **Houdini's wife:** Bess and the struggling magician married after only a few weeks of courtship.
- **The first hint of fame:** A savvy manager named Martin Beck gave Houdini some good advice and his first big break.

Around 1891, when Ehrich was seventeen years old, he quit his main job at the clothing factory to dedicate himself full-time to his career in magic. Ehrich joined with his friend Jacob Hyman to form a duo of magicians they called "The Brothers Houdini." The name Houdini came from an alteration of Ehrich's hero, the French magician Robert-Houdin. Ehrich, whose nickname was "Ehrie," morphed his first name into Harry. Harry Houdini was born.

Some biographers speculate that Ehrich invented the persona of Harry Houdini as an alter ego that had the power to escape from the terrible poverty and anti-Jewish rhetoric that had filled his childhood. They believe that he was driven to develop an omnipotent character that couldn't be contained by any force because of this deep urge to escape the powerlessness he experienced as a child. Whatever the real reasons, Ehrich, now Harry Houdini, began practicing his magic tricks several hours a day. He bought and read every book about magic that he could find. He learned that all handcuffs could be opened with a small number of keys and started practicing escaping from ropes with the help of a knowledgeable friend.

The actual members of the Brothers Houdini fluctuated. Jacob Hyman, discouraged by the lack of success of the show, quit the duo. Jacob's brother Joe Hyman replaced him for a while, but eventually quit as well. Houdini recruited his own younger brother Theodore, whom everyone called Dash. Dash looked like a huskier version of Houdini. Houdini was decidedly the boss of the duo. Their show consisted of card tricks and sleight of hand, but the major act was a trick Houdini called "Metamorphosis." This trick had become possible when Houdini purchased equipment from a retiring magician, after borrowing the needed money from Dash. The equipment included a trunk with a hidden escape hatch.

Performers normally used the trunk to lock themselves in, and then appear at another part of the theater. Houdini combined this trick idea with his developing ability to perform escapes. With his hands bound behind his back, Houdini was tied in a sack and put in the trunk. His assistant, Dash, drew some curtains around the trunk and announced a miracle on the count of three. Upon reaching the number three, the curtains were parted and Houdini stood outside of the trunk, untied. Inside the trunk, which Houdini now opened, was a tied sack containing Dash, whose hands were now tied behind his back.

Despite the success that other performers enjoyed with the trunk trick, the Brothers Houdini failed to draw big crowds. They usually performed as opening acts for other artists in dime museums and beer halls, making only the money that people threw into a hat. At the suggestion of a friend, Houdini tried polishing up his speech, changing the street slang he normally used to more formal, grammatically correct English. Despite not having gone to school full time as a child, Houdini had grown up with a very educated father from whom he had inherited a love of books and education. But still, the Brothers Houdini failed to have any real success.

In 1894, right around the time that his father died, Houdini met a petite, dark-haired girl named Wilhelmina Beatrice Rahner. Raised in a family of German Catholic immigrants, Wilhelmina was born in Brooklyn and went by the nickname Bess. Bess was a performer who sang and danced in a group called the Floral Sisters. Dash reportedly met her first during a performance and introduced her to Houdini. Houdini and Bess married after only two or three weeks of courtship and went to Coney Island for their honeymoon. Houdini was twenty and Bess was eighteen. Bess's mother objected to the marriage because Houdini was Jewish while Bess's family was Catholic, and Bess and her mother became estranged. Houdini and Bess took some time to get used to each other. Houdini was horrified to learn that Bess believed in many superstitions which he regarded as nonsense, and Bess had to cope with her husband's odd habits and intense work ethic, which allowed him to only sleep five hours a night.

Houdini quickly ejected Dash from the magic act and made Bess his partner; he and Bess became "The Houdinis." Bess's small size and pretty, expressive features enhanced the act, and Metamorphosis began to attract some attention. The Houdinis continued to perform in dime museums, doing up to fourteen acts a day. Houdini also tried to earn some money by selling short publications explaining various magic tricks. The Houdinis traveled around to various circuses and shows, and Houdini formed long-term friendships with other performers, individuals with physical oddities who made their living as "freaks."

Houdini later claimed that Bess changed his luck. But the early career of the Houdinis was grueling and low paying; Houdini and Bess worked contract to contract with various performing shows, often traveling with few amenities and sleeping on cots in bunks shared with other performers. The two tried several versions of their act, including a comedy show billed under Bess's maiden name, "The Rahners." Houdini and Bess sometimes doubled as other actors as needed, including stints as the Wild Man and a singing clown, respectively.

Police Escape Publicity Stunts

Houdini bought a share in a burlesque show known as "the Gaiety Girls," and Bess and Houdini traveled with the show through New York, Pennsylvania, and New England. Trying to create publicity for the shows, Houdini began showing up at local police stations and challenging police officials to find handcuffs from which he could not escape. After first attracting great attention with this performance while in Woonsocket, Rhode Island, Houdini repeated it at police stations all over New England. Police would secure him with up to six pairs of handcuffs at once, and Houdini would duck into a private room and emerge with the handcuffs open in under a minute.

The burlesque company eventually went bankrupt, but Houdini continued his escape stunts to promote whatever shows with which he was performing. In New Brunswick, Canada, police cuffed Houdini with sophisticated leather cuffs used to restrain patients in insane asylums. Houdini escaped within a few minutes. In Grand Rapids, Michigan, the sheriff clamped him in iron cuffs. Houdini was able to get out of them to great fanfare. In Chicago, he met challenges that he was hiding impressions of the jail's locks by offering to strip naked for his escape. The police accepted this challenge, locking Houdini's clothes in another cell. Houdini appeared mere moments later, fully dressed. Houdini's name made the papers that night, and this trick became known as the Nude Cell Escape. Houdini did experience a defeat shortly afterwards in Chicago, as the handcuffs put on him had been tampered with so that they would not open. Some biographers point out that Houdini's willingness to bare his body and the public's fascination with this trick might point to an element of eroticism in Houdini's appeal.

While touring with a medicine show in Kansas, Houdini tried a new moneymaking tactic, that of "speaking to the spirits." Spiritualism was a growing trend, with crowds paying conjurers to speak with their dead. Houdini, recognizing the simple tricks used to deceive naïve crowds into thinking that their deceased loved ones were reaching out from beyond the grave, made money with these performances, but soon abandoned them. He felt it was wrong to take advantage of vulnerable people who were mourning the loss of family and friends.

While Houdini enjoyed periodic flashes of fame due to his escapes from police stations, and the Houdini's performance of "Metamorphosis" was often a show-closer, he and Bess remained poor and relatively unknown. In 1898, the Houdinis returned to New York, exhausted from life on the road. While staying with his mother, Houdini, desperate to make a living that didn't involve the beer hall circuit, created a catalog for a magic school, in which he offered to teach pupils his escape tricks. Seriously considering getting out of the magic performance business, the Houdinis went to the Chicago area in December of 1898 to fulfill some previously agreed-to contracts. While performing in a beer hall in Saint Paul, Minnesota, Houdini was discovered by Martin Beck, a powerful manager who ran a circuit of vaudeville theaters.

Houdini's First Year of Fame

Martin Beck was a big name in the vaudeville circuit, booking for a group of major theaters known as the Orpheum Circuit. Vaudeville was a popular form of entertainment for middle-class American families of the time, consisting of shows performed in nice theaters, for which tickets were somewhat costly. A show usually consisted of eight to ten novelty acts, including acrobats, comedy routines, and a variety of talent and magic demonstrations. Vaudeville was considered a classier form of entertainment than that found in beer halls and dime museums, and a tour with a vaudeville show involved staying for one to two weeks at the same theater, performing only twice a day. For Houdini and Bess, who were accustomed to constant travel and performing up to fourteen times a day, performing in vaudeville was a luxurious life.

Houdini's brother Dash later credited Martin Beck as being the manager who made Houdini famous. Originally a German actor, Beck had become the owner of several vaudeville theaters. He excelled at recognizing not only talent but also at knowing how to present it to audiences. Beck also was able to manage Houdini's mercurial moods and frequently unreasonable demands. As he told Houdini from the beginning, he was determined to make Houdini a big name. He recommended that Houdini ditch his card tricks and smaller illusions and focus on performing his escapes. Houdini rearranged his act to include a needle-swallowing trick, Metamorphosis, and various innovative escape tricks, including escapes from thumb-cuffs, leg irons, and double-springed handcuffs. He continued to challenge police in stations around the country to try to restrain him inside their cells and in their best cuffs, agreeing to be stripped naked, searched, and to have his mouth taped shut in order to prove that he wasn't hiding any tools. In San Francisco he challenged local officials to place him in a straitjacket, the formidable reverse coat used to restrain criminally insane individuals. He escaped in less than ten minutes. Often Houdini's body was left bloody and bruised from the contortions and exertions of these escapes, but Houdini's trademark determination prevailed over these small injuries.

Beck made good on his promise to take care of Houdini. Beck steadily increased Houdini's salary and made careful plans for the development of his fame around the country and the world. Houdini, who had been making next to nothing on the beer hall circuit, began under Beck at sixty dollars a week, advancing to almost four hundred dollars a week by the end of his first year under Beck's management. At that time, that amount of money made Houdini a very rich man. He bought Bess extravagant gifts and sent money home to his mother, to whom he was devoted.

Houdini continued the rigorous daily practice of his tricks and hunted for new innovations. His ego also grew. He began to have serious disagreements with Martin Beck, scoffing at the percentage of profits that Beck took and complaining about lower-paying gigs that Beck had booked before Houdini achieved great fame. Beck managed Houdini's ego well. He did not back down in the face of Houdini's ungrateful demands. Beck planned a European tour for Houdini, followed by a return to the States, where he wanted Houdini finally to become recognized in New York City.

While in Europe, Houdini filled out a passport application, reporting that he had been born in Appleton, Wisconsin. Many biographers say that this fiction was symbolic of Harry Houdini's goal of erasing his poverty-stricken childhood as the child of a disadvantaged immigrant family.

Know More About: Vaudeville

Vaudeville began in the last decades of the nineteenth century. It grew out of other types of variety shows such as medicine shows, burlesque acts, and minstrel shows, among others. It was short-lived, lasting only into the early part of the twentieth century.

Vaudeville was characterized by its diversity. Each "show" held a variety of acts. It had dialogues (short, often comical, plays), juggling, pantomime, singing, jokes, dancing, contortion acts, and many other performances.

Houdini's magic act, especially in its early stages, fit in as well as anything in the hodgepodge environment of vaudeville. His later tricks, which required more time to complete and strange settings (such as a bridge or boiler) would not have fit in. Neither would Houdini's ego have worked well in vaudeville had it survived as a popular form of entertainment. As he grew more famous, he became more interested in being the star of the show. But, for a start, vaudeville allowed him to hone his talents and become familiar with performing for an audience. It also allowed him access to professional performers.

III. Houdini, the King of Handcuffs

Read It and Know It

After reading this chapter, you will know more about

- **The Nude Cell Escape:** Part magic, part scandalous nudity, this trick performed in police stations helped Houdini drum up publicity.
- **Early lawsuits:** When Houdini sued a newspaper for slander, a lucky break might have ensured his victory.
- **Houdini's disdain for imitators:** Not satisfied with being the best, Houdini often humiliated magicians who claimed his prowess with handcuffs for themselves.
- **The international view of Houdini:** Germany loved him, Paris was ambivalent, and Russia allowed him despite strong anti-Semitic sentiments.

Houdini arrived in London believing that bookings were waiting for him. He was enraged to find out that the international agent that Beck referred him to had failed to have anything ready. Houdini set out to drum up publicity by challenging the Scotland Yard police to confine him. He managed to get himself booked at the famous London theatre the Alhambra. London audiences loved his act, and Houdini quickly became famous there. However, he had to work harder to spread his fame into the English countryside, as the managers of theaters at various villages felt that his magic act did not fit what the family audiences of the time wanted. Houdini doggedly performed auditions for managers, until word of his unique tricks spread and he became a headliner in the country villages as well. He also advertised himself by performing the Nude Cell Escape at police stations in the small villages of the countryside. In one particularly famous performance in Sheffield, Houdini escaped from the high security unit where one of London's most famous murderers, Charles Pace, had been imprisoned.

For Houdini's onstage performances, he wore the formal dress of the time: a stiff, high collar, a white dickey, and a black dress coat. Bess frequently assisted him, wearing black knickerbockers. Houdini's brother Dash sometimes assisted as well or instead. Frequently there was a physician contracted to be backstage or onstage in case of emergency. Houdini performed his handcuff escapes behind a curtain, over which the audience could sometimes see his head, or else in a "cabinet" or "ghost house," a construction made to conceal Houdini's techniques from the audience.

Houdini's stage manner was something he studied and practiced almost as much as his magic. He worked hard to engage the audience and win them over to his side, presenting tricks with careful showmanship. He frequently made jokes that seemed self-deprecating, while also carefully building the tension in his audience members to keep them spellbound. He involved the audience in every way possible, an original tactic at the time.

In 1901 Houdini arranged with Beck to be let out of his contract. He became his own manager. In 1902, he introduced a new trick: the Packing Case Escape. A packing case was essentially a large crate that merchants of the time used for shipping. This act was a twist on the Metamorphosis trick. Houdini would arrange for a local store to provide the crate, and then would have assistants nail him into the crate onstage. Inspectors selected from the audience would verify its complete closing. The secret to Houdini's escape involved his ability to noiselessly disassemble the crate from the inside; Bess or another ally would direct the nailing shut of the crate such that one wall of the crate was less enforced. Many nails would be hammered into the top of the crate, creating the impression that it was sealed very tight all around. But, since Houdini did not come out of the top of the crate, this did not affect his ability to escape. Audiences loved this trick, and in one particular performance in Glasgow, Scotland at the Zoo-Hippodrome theatre, the crowd filled the theater and the streets outside to see it.

As part of his publicity campaign, Houdini frequently offered a reward to the public to anyone who could cuff him so that he could not escape. He did specify that he would only be cuffed by regulation, unaltered equipment. One experience that haunted him occurred in the working-class city of Blackburn, England. There, a young body-builder by the name of Hodgson challenged him to escape from powerful cuffs with which he had tampered. Goaded by the young man's scorn, Houdini accepted the challenge despite the tampering. Hodgson, who was knowledgeable about anatomy, cuffed Houdini in a torturous way that cut off his circulation and caused great pain. After fifteen minutes of working on the cuffs, Houdini explained that his circulation had been cut off and asked Hodgson to allow him a break from the cuffs for it to return. Hodgson refused. Houdini returned to the torturous struggle, and after almost two hours, emerged free from restraints, his body bloody and torn.

Hodgson, however, scorned Houdini's efforts in a public interview shortly after the performance, saying that he had evidence that Houdini had cut himself out of the cuffs with the help of Bess and his brother Dash, who were onstage with him. Enraged, Houdini changed his plans so that he could return to Blackburn to rebut these charges. Even though he returned to Blackburn on later tours, he always faced Hodgson-supporters who booed him while onstage and challengers who tried to defeat him using damaged cuffs.

In perhaps one of his most-talked-about escapes, a representative from the *London Daily Mirror*, a popular newspaper, came onstage during one of Houdini's performances and told him of a famous pair of handcuffs made by a British blacksmith. The handcuffs had taken the blacksmith five years to make, and were probably the most sophisticated restraints in existence at the time. Only one person, a famous lock-picker, had ever been able to open the cuffs, a feat that took him forty-four hours. Houdini accepted the challenge to escape from these cuffs, and the event was scheduled to take place four days later at a major London theater called the Hippodrome.

When the night finally arrived, the Hippodrome was packed. Houdini explained that he wasn't sure if he was going to be able to open the cuffs, but that he would try his best. He disappeared behind the curtain, appearing once after twenty-two minutes to look at the cuffs in a better light and again after another thirteen minutes to ask for a glass of water. The house manager gave Houdini a cushion to sit on because Houdini reported that his knees were hurting. Houdini disappeared back behind the curtain. After an hour of working on the cuffs, he came out from behind the curtain, looking so disheveled and exhausted that some say that Bess became overwhelmed with emotion and had to leave the theater. He asked to be unlocked just to take off his coat, as he was perspiring heavily. The *Mirror* representative refused to uncuff him unless he admitted defeat. Frustrated and defiant, Houdini managed to get a penknife out of his shirt pocket with his mouth, which he used to cut the coat to shreds, removing it. The audience went crazy. Ten minutes later, Houdini emerged from behind the curtain, uncuffed.

Modern magicians and biographers believe that Houdini must have arranged this trick in collaboration with the *Daily Mirror* in order to gain publicity for both. Lock experts say that there is no way that the cuffs could have been opened without a key, and that Bess must have brought one to Houdini in the glass of water, or else it was put in the cushion that was given to him. Many believe that Houdini designed the famous cuffs himself, and simply waited an hour behind the curtain, coming out to demand water and to cut himself out of the coat for effect. In any case, the performance made Houdini the talk of London for a long time, and Houdini fanned the flame of this publicity by offering one hundred guineas to anyone who could escape the same handcuffs. One young man with exceptionally small hands who could have maneuvered out of the cuffs accepted this challenge, but was stumped when Houdini simply asked him to open the cuffs without being cuffed. By the end of his time at the Hippodrome, worn down from excitement and work, Houdini became ill with a cold that had him in bed for twelve days.

Germany and Paris

In order to perform in Germany, Houdini had to pass a rigorous inspection by the police. At the time, Germany had an authoritarian government, and entertainers were required to check all acts with law enforcement officials in order to be allowed to perform. Many entertainers were prosecuted and jailed for fraud on the public if their acts were in any way based on myth. Stripped naked and cuffed in the police station, Houdini was able to open the cuffs under the screen of a blanket in front of police, who admitted that they did not know how he had done it.

Houdini got permission to perform but soon faced another problem when a newspaper published an article claiming that he had bribed a police officer in order to make his escape. Houdini hired a lawyer and brought a lawsuit for slander. He could only win the case by revealing some of his secrets. He demonstrated how he banged on a lock until the spring weakened and it opened, and took the judge to the side of the room and showed him how he got out of handcuffs. Some biographers say that the judge brought Houdini to his back office and told him that he must open the judge's safe in order to prove that he wasn't a fraud, but that the safe had been left open, by sheer luck. In any case, Houdini won the suit, and the newspaper published an apology. In police-controlled Germany, Houdini's ability to escape physical restraints and willingness to challenge authority made him something of a hero and a symbol of freedom and liberty to the German people.

While in Germany, Houdini attempted to interview a famous retired magician named Wiljalba Frikell, who had done more performances than any other magician. At first the man refused to see Houdini, as he believed that Houdini was really his illegitimate son that had come to confront him. Eventually Frikell agreed to meet with Houdini but died of a heart attack a mere two hours before Houdini was scheduled to arrive.

Houdini continued to encourage challengers to try to restrain him and to face imitators, whom he went out of his way to humiliate by showing up at their performances and cuffing them in restraints from which they could not escape.

Overall, German people worshipped Houdini, and he enjoyed his time there. He spoke a little bit of German, as his father had spoken it in his childhood home, and endeared himself to the German public by trying to communicate in that language. He brought his mother, whom he was fully supporting financially, to Germany to visit for one summer, and reportedly bought her a dress that had been worn by the late Queen Victoria.

Houdini had more limited success in Paris; the police there did not allow him to perform escapes from some of the famous military prisons, and he received good but brief reviews. He did take advantage of his time in France to attempt to visit the surviving family of Robert-Houdin, the famous French magician whom Houdini worshipped and after whom he had named himself. Robert-Houdin's daughter-in-law refused to allow him to visit, and when Houdini went to the house anyway, refused to allow him inside. Instead, Houdini went to the nearby cemetery where Robert-Houdin's grave was located and paid his respects, staying by the grave for half an hour.

Paris was also where Houdini made his first foray into acting in a brief film called the *Merveilleux Exploits du Celebre Houdini a Paris.*

Russia

In spring of 1903 Houdini was booked to perform in Moscow, Russia. At the time the country's authoritarian government maintained oppressive control over the population and demanded that people carry internal passports to travel from one place in the country to another. The government heavily employed censorship tactics in order to keep control over the country's citizens, and the police spied on citizens' activities at all times.

In addition, there was an intense anti-Semitic sentiment. During Houdini's time there, violence against Jews was increasing. Houdini went to visit the site of a massacre of Jews in the Russian town of Kishinev, horrified and offended at the violence against his people. Biographers are amazed that Houdini was even allowed to perform in Moscow, as at the time Jews were not allowed into Russia. Houdini did not enjoy the culture of Russia, finding the people very superstitious and "backwards." He did reportedly claim a victory by escaping a "Siberian Transport Carette"—a large portable cell used to transport prisoners to Siberia. He also performed for Grand Duke Sergei Alexandrovich and the duchess at the Palace Kleinmichel, performing his needle-swallowing act. Houdini performed in his rudimentary version of the Russian language, which improved with practice.

Know More About: Robert-Houdin

Jean Eugene Robert was born in 1805 in Blois, France. He was a clockmaker (a family business) before becoming the "father of modern magic." His name acquired the hyphenated "Houdin" when he married Josephe Cecile Houdin. His wife was also from a clock making family, and it is thought that he added her name for business reasons.

He was famous for using electricity in his performances and for his act "Second Sight." In this act he would blindfold his son, then hold up objects for his son to identify. It is generally agreed that Robert-Houdin used a talking code for this trick. Indeed, a part of *The Unmasking of Robert-Houdin* by Houdini is dedicated to explaining that not only did Robert-Houdin not invent the act "Second Sight," but also how the talking code or other audio signals were used to perform it.

The father of modern magic wrote *Memoirs of Robert-Houdin, Ambassador, Author, and Conjurer* in 1859. It is in this book he claimed to have invented "Second Sight" with the following story:

My two children were playing one day in the drawing-room at a game they had invented for their own amusement. The younger had bandaged his elder brother's eyes, and made him guess the objects he touched, and when the latter happened to guess right, they changed places. This simple game suggested to me the most complicated idea that ever crossed my mind.

Pursued by the notion, I ran and shut myself up in my workroom, and was fortunately in that happy state when the mind follows easily the combinations traced by fancy. I rested my head in my hands, and, in my excitement, laid down the first principles of second sight.

Despite Houdini's later contempt of Robert-Houdin's claims, there is no doubt that the older magician was very famous and admired by many. Robert-Houdin lived until 1871.

In Houdini's Words

Houdini immortalized the famous not-quite meeting between himself and Frikell in the introduction to The Unmasking of Robert-Houdin.

I had heard that Frikell and not Robert-Houdin was the first magician to discard cumbersome, draped stage apparatus, and to don evening clothes, and I was most anxious to verify this rumor, as well as to interview him regarding equally important data bearing on the history of magic. Having heard that he lived in Kötchenbroda, a suburb of Dresden, I wrote to him from Cologne, asking for an interview. I received in reply a curt note: "Herr verreist," meaning "The master is on tour." This, I knew, from his age, could not be true, so I took a week off for personal investigation. I arrived at Kötchenbroda on the morning of April 8th, 1903, at 4 o'clock, and was directed to his home, known as "Villa Frikell." Having found my bearings and studied well the exterior of the house, I returned to the depot to await daylight. At 8:30 I reappeared at his door, and was told by his wife that Herr Frikell had gone away.

I then sought the police department from which I secured the following information: "Dr." Wiljalba Frikell was indeed the retired magician whom I was so anxious to meet. He was eighty-seven years old, and in 1884 had celebrated his golden anniversary as a conjurer. Living in the same town was an adopted daughter, but she could not or would not assist me. The venerable magician had suffered from domestic disappointments and had made a vow that he would see no one. In fact he was leading a hermit-like life.

Armed with this information, I employed a photographer, giving him instructions to post himself opposite the house and make a snap shot of the magician, should he appear in the doorway. But I had counted without my host. All morning the photographer lounged across the street and all morning I stood bareheaded before the door of Herr Frikell, pleading with his wife who leaned from the window overhead. With that peculiar fervency which comes only when the heart's desire is at stake, I begged that the past master of magic would lend a helping hand to one ready to sit at his feet and learn. I urged the debt which he owed to the literature of magic and which he could pay by giving me such direct information as I needed for my book.

Frau Frikell heard my pleadings with tears running down her cheeks, and later I learned that Herr Frikell also listened to them, lying grimly on the other side of the shuttered window.

At length, yielding to physical exhaustion, I went away, but I was still undaunted. I continued to bombard Herr Frikell with letters, press clippings regarding my work, etc., and finally in Russia I received a letter from him. I might send him a package containing a certain brand of Russian tea of which he was particularly fond. You may be sure I lost no time in shipping the little gift, and shortly I was rewarded by the letter for which I longed. Having decided that I cared more for him than did some of his relatives, he would receive me when next I played near Kötchenbroda.

With this interview in prospect, I made the earliest engagement obtainable in Dresden, intending to give every possible moment to my hardly-won acquaintance. But Fate interfered. One business problem after another arose, concerning my forthcoming engagement in England, and I had to postpone my visit to Herr Frikell until the latter part of the week. In the mean time, he had agreed to visit a Dresden photographer, as I wanted an up-to-date photograph of him and he had only pictures taken in his more youthful days. On the day when he came to Dresden for his sitting, he called at the theatre, but the attachés, without informing me, refused to give him the name of the hotel where I was stopping.

After the performance I dropped into the König Kaffe and was much annoyed by the staring and gesticulations of an elderly couple at a distant table. It was Frikell with his wife, but I did not recognize them and, not being certain on his side, he failed to make himself known. That was mid-week, and for Saturday, which fell on October 8th, 1903, I had an engagement to call at the Villa Frikell. On Thursday, the Central Theatre being sold out to Cleo de Merode, who was playing special engagements in Germany with her own company, I made a flying business trip to Berlin, and on my return I passed through Kötchenbroda. As the train pulled into the station I hesitated. Should I drop off and see Herr Frikell, or wait for my appointment on the morrow? Fate turned the wheel by a mere thread and I went on to Dresden. So does she often dash our fondest hopes!

My appointment for Saturday was at 2 P.M., and as my train landed me in Kötchenbroda a trifle too early I walked slowly from the depot to the Villa Frikell, not wishing to disturb my aged host by arriving ahead of time.

I rang the bell. It echoed through the house with peculiar shrillness. The air seemed charged with a quality which I presumed was the intense pleasure of realizing my long cherished hope of meeting the great magician. A lady opened the door and greeted me with the words: "You are being waited for."

I entered. He was waiting for me indeed, this man who had consented to meet me, after vowing that he would never again look into the face of a stranger. And Fate had forced him to keep that vow. Wiljalba Frikell was dead. The body, clad in the best his wardrobe afforded, all of which had been donned in honor of his expected guest, was not yet cold. Heart failure had come suddenly and unannounced. The day before he had cleaned up his souvenirs in readiness for my coming and arranged a quantity of data for me. On the wall above the silent form were all of his gold medals, photographs taken at various stages of his life, orders presented to him by royalty—all the outward and visible signs of a vigorous, active, and successful life, the life of which he would have told me, had I arrived ahead of Death. And when all these were arranged, he had forgotten his morbid dislike of strangers. The old instincts of hospitality tugged at his heart strings, and his wife said he was almost young and happy once more, when suddenly he grasped at his heart, crying, "My heart! What is the matter with my heart? O——" That was all!

There we stood together, the woman who had loved the dear old wizard for years and the young magician who would have been so willing to love him had he been allowed to know him. His face was still wet from the cologne she had thrown over him in vain hope of reviving the fading soul. On the floor lay the cloths, used so ineffectually to bathe the pulseless face, and now laughing mockingly at one who saw himself defeated after weary months of writing and pleading for the much-desired meeting.

IV. Houdini, Back in the United States

Read It and Know It

After reading this chapter, you will know more about

- **New acts:** The Milk Can Escape and the Manacled Bridge Jump would increase Houdini's fame in the U.S.
- **Dash:** Houdini's brother styled himself the Magician Hardeen and set himself up as Houdini's rival, probably to increase Houdini's fame.
- **Houdini's challenge to the public:** When Houdini announced he could escape from anything, companies met his challenge by putting him in a vise, a giant envelope, and mailbags.
- **The iron boiler:** When Houdini nearly failed to escape this dangerous container, his fame only grew.

After four and half years abroad, Houdini returned to the United States in the summer of 1905, intending to work for only six weeks before returning to Europe for a final tour and then retiring. He bought a country estate in Stamford, Connecticut and a townhouse in Harlem, into which he moved his mother, sister, and two of his brothers. His brother Leo was now a physician and ran the household while Houdini completed magic shows around the country. The house was located at 278 West 113th Street, and is commonly referred to as 278.

Houdini's past unsuccessful career in the United States was hardly known, but American audiences now knew him as the King of Handcuffs who had wowed Europe. Determined to keep his fame skyrocketing, Houdini began to work on yet more amazing tricks. He began practicing swimming and holding his breath under water. He had a special large, deep bathtub installed at 278, where Bess would time him as he held his breath under the water. He also practiced exposing himself to cold water. These exercises were preparation for two new acts: the Milk Can Escape and the Manacled Bridge Jump.

In the Milk Can Escape, Houdini climbed into a large can filled with water. The top of the can was closed and locked with at least six padlocks. The can was covered from view by curtains. A huge stopwatch was placed on the stage, and the audience was invited to try to hold its breath as long as Houdini had to in order to escape from the can. An assistant stood by with an ax, ready to break open the can "in case something went wrong." Of course, no audience member could hold his or her breath for the two minutes that it took Houdini to emerge from the can. The curtains opened to a free Houdini, and the crowd could see that the padlocks on the top of the can were still intact. The secret of the escape is known to other magicians and is purely mechanical in nature.

In Houdini's other stunt, the Manacled Bridge Jump (also known as the Underwater Handcuff Release), Houdini himself admitted that he was doing something dangerous. This trick involved a handcuffed Houdini leaping from high bridges into rivers below and emerging from the water unshackled. He debuted this trick on film in Rochester, New York and repeated it in the Mississippi River in New Orleans, the Detroit River, the Allegheny River in Pittsburgh, and the Charles River in Boston, from the Harvard Bridge. At least one imitator died doing this trick.

Houdini also continued his nude cell escapes, his most famous of this era being from the high-security prison in Washington that had been designed specifically to hold President Garfield's assassin, Charles Guiteau. Houdini not only escaped Guiteau's cell, but also let the other eight prisoners in the other cells of the jail out, convinced them to swap cells, locked them back in, retrieved his clothes, and arrived in the main foyer of the prison.

Houdini arranged for his brother Dash, now the magician Hardeen, to follow him to America and again be his closest rival. It is unclear how much of the rivalry, which was played out in boasts each made to the press, was staged and how much was real.

While performing in the States, Houdini opened up his biggest challenge to the public yet: essentially, that he could escape from anything, at anytime. The public rose to meet this challenge. A Pennsylvania tool company challenged Houdini to escape from their strong vises, a Chicago envelope company designed a huge envelope for him to escape from, and the United States Postal Services provided him with mailbags from which to escape. The list goes on and on. In an escape from automobile chains made by the Weed Tire Chain Grip Company, Houdini took nearly twenty minutes to get out and emerged exhausted and speechless.

In 1906 Houdini orchestrated three escapes in the city of Boston that had the city's residents spellbound. In the first of the escapes, he was triple-handcuffed inside a rattan hamper. In the second, he broke out of the city jail, somehow eluding police stationed at the three exits, and called them blocks away from the theater to let them know that he'd left. In the third performance, at Harvard University, students tied him with over sixty feet of rope, from which he escaped in around twelve minutes. Houdini also performed his needle-swallowing trick for a group of Boston physicians.

The following year, 1907, Houdini returned to Boston for another daredevil trick: an escape from an iron boiler made by a Cambridge manufacturer. The trick did not go as planned, and Houdini took nearly an hour to escape, emerging bloody and trembling. His fame in Boston reached a huge climax.

V. Houdini, the Aviator

Read It and Know It

After reading this chapter, you will know more about

- **Houdini and the sea:** Able to escape from handcuffs even underwater, Houdini nonetheless suffered from seasickness.
- **Houdini's obsession:** He didn't just want to learn to fly; he wanted to be the first in the country.
- **Accidental fame:** Although Houdini never intended to perform in Australia, the desire to fly brought him to the island continent where the tricks he performed to support his new obsession made him popular.
- **Houdini's "flight"iness:** After only a few years, Houdini was bored with flying and sold his plane.

Despite having vowed to never perform in Australia, Houdini found himself on his way to that continent on a ship called the Malwa in 1910. Houdini, who always got very seasick when traveling by boat, reportedly lost twenty-five pounds on the trip. He was determined, however, to reach Australian shores because of a new obsession: flying airplanes. In 1909 the first flights around the world were taking place, and Houdini immediately became obsessed with aviation. He bought himself a plane in Hamburg, Germany and rented the services of a plane mechanic named Brassac. Houdini began to train with Brassac in Hamburg and then in Paris. He was determined to become the first man in flight in Australia.

On February 6, 1909 the ship finally reached Australia. Houdini exhausted himself by continuing to perform his magic shows while keeping a rigorous flying practice schedule. Others on the Australian continent were getting close to getting into the air, and Houdini wanted to be the first. On the morning of March 18, he took three successful flights. A day earlier, another amateur aeronaut had also taken flight but didn't reach an altitude high enough to technically have completed what officials called a flight. Perhaps troubled by this possible challenge to his record, Houdini kept taking more and riskier flights, with more and more spectators coming to watch.

While in Australia, Houdini performed his manacled bridge dives and became a celebrity there as well. He was able to obtain ringside seats to boxing matches, boxing being one of his passions.

In May of 1910 Houdini finally packed up his plane and headed back to New York. Houdini kept up with aviation in the United States, watching professional aviators take flights that were beyond his reach just a few years ago in Australia. In 1913 Houdini sold his plane and announced that he was done with flying.

In Houdini's Words

Houdini's experience in Australia was not limited to flying, as mentioned above. While there he traveled and performed. As always, he sought to improve his performance and explore the methods of other performers. In *Miracle Mongers and Their Methods* Houdini describes a story he became familiar with about the experience of the Australian traveler. His tone in this passage helps us to discover some of his thoughts about the island continent he was so reluctant to visit.

I will here relate the story of a sad death—I might feel inclined to call it suicide—which occurred in Melbourne shortly before my arrival in the colonies. About a year previous to the time of which I am now writing, a gentleman of birth and education, a Cambridge B. A., a barrister by profession and a literary man by choice, with his wife and three children emigrated to Victoria. He arrived in Melbourne with one hundred and fifty pounds in his pocket, and hope unlimited in his heart.

Poor man! He, like many another man, quickly discovered that muscles in Australia are more marketable than brains. His little store of money began to melt under the necessities of his wife and family. To make matters worse he was visited by a severe illness. He was confined to his bed for some weeks, and during his convalescence his wife presented him with another of those "blessings to the poor man," a son.

It was Christmas time, his health was thoroughly restored, he naturally possessed a vigorous constitution; but his heart was beginning to fail him, and his funds were sinking lower and lower.

At last one day, returning from a long and solitary walk, he sat down with pen and paper and made a calculation by which he found he had sufficient money left to pay the insurance upon his life for one year, which, in the case of his death occurring within that time, would bring to his widow the sum of three thousand pounds. He went to the insurance office, and made his application—was examined by the doctor—the policy was made out, his life was insured. From that day he grew moody and morose, despair had conquered hope.

At this time a snake-charmer came to Melbourne, who advertised a wonderful cure for snake-bites. This charmer took one of the halls in the town, and there displayed his live stock, which consisted of a great number of the most deadly and venomous snakes which were to be found in India and Australia.

This man had certainly some most wonderful antidote to the poison of a snake's fangs. In his exhibitions he would allow a cobra to bite a dog or a rabbit, and, in a short time after he had applied his nostrum the animal would thoroughly revive; he advertised his desire to perform upon humanity, but, of course, he could find no one would be fool enough to risk his life so unnecessarily.

The advertisement caught the eye of the unfortunate emigrant, who at once proceeded to the hall where the snake charmer was holding his exhibition. He offered himself to be experimented upon; the fanatic snake-charmer was delighted, and an appointment was made for the same evening as soon as the "show" should be over.

The evening came; the unfortunate man kept his appointment, and, in the presence of several witnesses, who tried to dissuade him from the trial, bared his arm and placed it in the cage of an enraged cobra and was quickly bitten. The nostrum was applied apparently in the same manner as it had been to the lower animals which had that evening been experimented upon, but whether it was that the poor fellow wilfully did something to prevent its taking *effect—or whatever the reason—he soon became insensible, and in a couple of hours he was taken home to his wife and family—a corpse. The next morning the snake-charmer had flown, and left his snakes behind him.*

The insurance company at first refused payment of the policy, asserting that the death was suicide; the case was tried and the company lost it, and the widow received the three thousand pounds. The snake-charmer was sought in vain; he had the good fortune and good sense to be seen no more in the Australian colonies.

VI. Houdini, the Evolving Magician and Illusionist

Read It and Know It

After reading this chapter, you will know more about

- **Houdini's new act:** Eschewing handcuff tricks, the magician focused on more daring escapes.
- **Early injuries:** As he grew older, Houdini's tricks began to take a physical toll.
- **The death of Cecilia:** When Houdini's mother passed, the magician was deeply grieved and had difficulty recovering.
- **Illusions:** Houdini used these tricks, which were growing in popularity, in astonishing ways.

Starting in 1910, Houdini announced that he would no longer do handcuff tricks. To replace these stunts, Houdini turned to even more daring and complex acts: the Underwater Box Escape, the Crazy-Crib, and the Chinese Water Torture Cell. In a forever-famous incident, Houdini scheduled an underwater escape in the East River of New York. However, the police prevented him from performing, so Houdini had a tugboat bring him out to federal waters. Once there, he was shackled and placed inside a thick pine box, with holes that allowed water and air to get in. The box was thrown over the side of the boat. Houdini managed to get out of the box and the shackles, climbing into the boat to great cheers. Houdini repeated this stunt in New York in 1914 in the waters off Battery Park, to great fanfare.

Houdini also performed escapes from restraints used to confine criminally insane individuals, including "crazy-cribs," which were lightweight beds with extensive straps. He invited more "one-time-only" challenges from the public, which lead to his escape from ropes in which he dangled from the Heidelberg Tower's roof in New York City. He also escaped from the belly of a huge sea creature found in Cape Cod, which was brought to a stage and chained closed after Houdini climbed inside.

Houdini additionally introduced escapes from torture chambers brought from around the world, including the Chinese sanguaw, the Scottish gibbet, and the German iron maiden torture chest. Houdini devised yet another, more complex torture chamber for himself: the Chinese Water Torture Cell, or the Upside Down (USD). In this device, Houdini was shackled upside down with his feet in stocks and lowered into a vat of water. The stocks were then closed with padlocks. Many people at the time believed that Houdini was only able to escape from the cell by using supernatural abilities to dematerialize and re-materialize. Only a few people in the world know how Houdini actually did this trick.

Houdini's years of constant, physical performances took a strain on his body. In 1911 he suffered his first lasting injury, a broken blood vessel in a kidney sustained when he was tied too tightly in one of his public challenges. The doctor told Houdini that he needed to stop his contortionist activities for good, but Houdini refused. He tore a ligament in his side soon after.

Houdini began to need help lugging around his huge amount of equipment. But he risked exposure of his secrets by employing assistants. He carefully selected helpers, whom he paid well and made take oaths of secrecy about what they learned about his magic. Even still, the assistants were never told the whole story behind any trick, just in case one were to betray him. Likely Dash and Bess were the only two people who knew how Houdini really pulled off his tricks.

In July of 1913 Houdini left for Europe again. He got word of his mother Cecilia's grave illness soon after arriving and headed straight back to her bedside. Unfortunately, Cecilia passed away before Houdini arrived, and Houdini returned to his European tour with a grieving heart.

In Nuremberg, Germany, he defied a court order that forbid him from performing the Chinese Water Torture Cell under the waters of a lake near Nuremberg; he was prosecuted by the police and won the case. Houdini was the only one who didn't seem to take pleasure in the ridiculous proceedings; he sat lost in grief in the courtroom. Houdini saw that his black mood was having a negative effect on Bess's health and resolved to bounce back. He took Bess on a vacation in the French Riviera but indulged in a morbid fascination with a cemetery there.

Houdini tried starting a new show based solely on illusions instead of on escape tricks, including an illusion invented by another magician, the Expanding Cube. Houdini performed this illusion by telling the audience that his wife was inside a small die, and then "making" the die expand, removing the enlarged item to reveal Bess, sitting on the platform. However, other performers also used this trick, and audiences wanted Houdini to perform his trademark escapes, not other magicians' illusions.

On a boat trip back to the United States, Houdini performed for an amazed President Theodore Roosevelt. A photograph of the president and eight men from the ship, including Houdini, was taken. Houdini had the other men in the picture airbrushed out and presented the photo of himself and Roosevelt to the public as the original photograph.

Houdini's next tour abroad was delayed by the breakout of World War I. He turned back to touring in the United States, still struggling with grief over the loss of his mother. He leased the house in Harlem that his mother had lived in for the last years of her life and turned to new tricks: walking through a brick wall, being buried alive, and, most famously, the Suspended Straitjacket Escape. His "walking through a brick wall" trick, in which he literally seemed to do what the trick's title indicates, made a big sensation but was quickly discarded by Houdini as too easy to replicate and too hard to orchestrate (one had to build a genuine brick wall for each show). In Los Angeles, he agreed to escape a six-foot deep grave, shackled by handcuffs. He reported later that he panicked and nearly died.

Houdini's crowning escapade of this era was being hung, upside down and straitjacketed, from tall buildings, far from the ground. Houdini first did this trick in Minneapolis from the building of the city newspaper, and he repeated it on skyscrapers in Omaha, San Antonio, New Orleans, New York, and Providence, among others. Huge crowds turned out to see this breathtaking stunt. This trick was as dangerous as it was attention grabbing. Several other performers died trying to replicate the feat; safety hazards lay in tangled ropes, fractures of ankles and necks from the upside-down position and heavy pulleys, and the risk of catching overhead wires or hitting a wall while struggling to get free. While performing in Oakland, Houdini met the famous writer Jack London and his wife Charmian, which produced another photo opportunity for Houdini to pose with a famous person and circulate the picture among friends and family.

In the fall of 1918, Houdini starred in a new variety show at the Hippodrome, called "Everything." Having shown himself to be very proud of being American at the break-out of the first world war, he continued his patriotic theme by buying an eagle named Young Abe, which he produced out of nowhere in a spectacular opening number. Houdini also performed his upside-down straitjacket escape, suspended high over the Hippodrome stage by wire.

Illusions

In his later career, Houdini introduced a new kind of magic, illusions. Houdini's illusion acts differed from his past stunts which showcased his physical prowess and mental skill at beating locks, chains, and all sorts of restraints, with the exception that Houdini had briefly introduced an illusion in which he appeared to walk through a brick wall. Like everything Houdini did, he did illusions in a big way. He procured an elephant named Jenny, who was reportedly the daughter of P.T. Barnum's circus elephant Jumbo.

Jenny weighed between four thousand and ten thousand pounds. Houdini made her disappear onstage during an eight-minute act in which the elephant appeared onstage, gave Houdini an elephant kiss, and was concealed briefly behind a screen. When the screen was lifted, two seconds later, Jenny had disappeared. Houdini purchased the international rights for this trick from its inventor, a British magician named Charles Morritt. This trick made huge news even though in actuality, only a small section of the audience in the huge Hippodrome theatre was actually positioned such that they could see the elephant and her disappearance. Houdini's showmanship and reputation, however, was such that the trick still became hugely famous, and Houdini maintained the satisfaction of staying on top of the world of magic. The illusion is still talked about today.

Houdini finally reached Broadway in 1925, while in his early fifties. His show HOUDINI was a three-act, two and a half hour show, featuring a whole hour of new illusions. The show toured at highbrow theaters around the country, and featured young, sexily clad female assistants, as well as Bess, her niece, and her niece's mother. Even after breaking a bone in his foot, Houdini continued to perform in HOUDINI, although unable to do the Chinese Water Torture Cell, as it involved hanging upside-down from his ankles.

Although by the mid-1920s Houdini had begun branching away from his more physically strenuous tricks, he returned to the arena when a young magician named Rahman Bey began performing a much-acclaimed show involving animal hypnotism and piercing himself with steel pins, tricks that Houdini had already revealed the methods of in his books (see Chapter VIII). Houdini resented the competition from Bey and that Bey claimed to go into a "cataleptic trance" that allowed him to perform these tricks. Another strike against Bey was that Houdini's enemy from his battle against fraudulent Spiritualist mediums, a man named Carrington (see Chapter XI), was the announcer of Bey's show.

But worst of all was Bey's claim to be able to remain in a casket underwater, without air, for long periods of time. Houdini publically announced that he could beat any record that Bey set for staying in a casket underwater. Although Bey had failed to stay underwater for more than twenty minutes during an attempt in which he was lowered into the Hudson River in a casket, Bey soon managed to remain in his underwater box for an hour in a pool in New York City. Houdini immediately began training to beat this record, obtaining a casket from the same company that made Bey's. After three weeks of training, Houdini beat Bey's record by staying submerged in his casket at New York's Sheldon Hotel's pool for an hour and a half, despite the temperature in the casket rising to heights not anticipated during Houdini's test runs. Houdini insisted that he did not use any special equipment or go into any trance to perform this feat, but rather that he had merely trained himself to breathe slowly.

VII. Houdini, the Man

Read It and Know It

After reading this chapter, you will know more about

- **Houdini's ego:** The magician's need to be on top often brought him trouble.
- **The marriage:** Houdini and Bess were private about their relationship, but most agree they had a loving, supportive marriage despite a likely affair.
- **The fulfilled promise:** The deathbed promise Houdini made to his father to care for Cecilia was one that Houdini took pleasure in fulfilling.
- **The Catholic mother-in-law:** Bess was reunited with her estranged mother after an illness.

Houdini's Inner Self

Houdini's obsession with self-promotion seemed to have started a young age. Pictures of him as a child and teenager show him posing for the camera, showing off his medals (some real, some fake) and his messenger uniform. He billed himself as "Eric, Prince of Air" at the young age of seven. By the time he died, Ehrich had turned himself into the all-powerful persona Houdini, attempting to leave behind even the first name "Harry" because he thought "Houdini" sounded more regal than "Harry Houdini." Even when not in the public eye, this character seemed important to him; his wife and family called him Houdini, and he had his initials HH embroidered on his pajamas and other personal items. His diary entries as well as his public statements reflect a strong propensity to twist the truth to flatter his ego and sense of importance.

Biographers attribute Houdini's desire to transform himself into an all-powerful, world-known figure as stemming from a need to escape his childhood of deprivation and insecurity. Other psychoanalysts have gone further to explain Houdini's obsession with escaping restraints and defying death as a reaction to an extreme Oedipal complex. Some also point out to the novelty of Houdini's nude jail cell escapes and speculate that Houdini's willingness to bare his body might point to an element of eroticism in Houdini's appeal.

Whatever the case, Houdini's personal writings reflect his anxiety to stay forever famous, his fears that his success would just be fleeting, and his desperation to stay on top. Despite his huge ego, he clearly always felt like he was about to become irrelevant, that he must crush all who threatened or opposed him before he himself got crushed, and that he might become poor again. Although rich, he carefully saved money in case of future poverty and scrimped money wherever he could, except for his extravagant spending on his collections and other passions. Although famous, he went out of his way to crush imitators and to sue any who tried to use his name. Although renowned throughout the world at a relatively early age, he continued seeking more dangerous and breathtaking stunts, often performing when injured and in pain.

Even though many could and did criticize Houdini's self-obsession, no one could attack his work ethic. Houdini trained for hours each day and stayed up into the night reading and researching to improve his performances and collections. It is rumored that he was an insomniac who used his long waking hours to further his professional goals. Even when Houdini took time off, he juggled several projects and was constantly on the go. He didn't seem to know any other pace besides flat out.

Ethnically Jewish, Houdini was proud of his educated rabbi father and raised money for Jewish organizations. He did not approve of indulging in alcohol or drugs, and also looked with contempt on men going to lewd shows and otherwise womanizing. He seemed apathetic towards politics and issues of social justice, although he did approve of steps towards racial equality that he witnessed in England. Having first come into fame in England, he considered himself as having more in common with the British and other European nations than with Americans. He proudly presented his shows in Germany and Russia in what he knew of those countries' languages. However, he made himself into an American citizen by falsifying his place of birth on his passport, changing it from Budapest, Hungary to Appleton, Wisconsin. He also claimed his birthdate was slightly different than the real date (April 6, 1874 instead of March 24, 1874). Further, when war broke out, he dove into patriotic efforts to raise money for the United States effort and to contribute his skills to raising the morale of the troops and the public.

Clearly an intelligent man, Houdini was keenly aware that his lack of formal education put him at a disadvantage.

Coming from a house filled with his father's books and love of learning, he yearned to be considered worthy of joining the ranks of academia and to be regarded as more than just a magician. This desire likely fed his passions for collecting books and for writing, as well as for making connections with famous authors such as Sir Arthur Conan Doyle and Jack London, as well as other academics such as Robert Gould Shaw. Despite his drive to be considered equal to those in the academic, elite world, Houdini reportedly cared very little about his appearance when off-stage, frequently appearing in rumpled and dirty clothes. He also maintained friendships with the usually lower-class circus and beer hall performers that he had worked with in his early career, and went out of his way to send flowers and gifts to the working-class people that had helped him and his family while he was growing up.

In his forties Houdini became known as a generous charity figure. He called his works of charity "Good Works" and received no payment for them. He had a particular reputation for handing out money to older people who were down on their luck, perhaps because they reminded him of his impoverished father. He performed shows at charity hospitals, orphanages, and prisons. Most famously, he put on a three-hour show at Sing Sing prison, much longer than his or any other magicians' of the times shows. Houdini interestingly commented that he thought that given a different set of circumstances, he himself might have found himself leading a criminal life.

Houdini and Bess

Despite Houdini's passion for publicity, his relationship with his wife Bess was kept private from the press. Observers frequently said that Houdini appeared to act very lovingly towards Bess, and after his death his property was found to contain many love notes written to her, describing her as his sunshine and using many other romantic metaphors. Bess, like Houdini, was very private. She liked to make clothes and fine food, and to shop. The couple did not have any children, despite their attempts to conceive. Their letters to friends reflect sadness that they were not able to have children. They parented instead their pets, which included a small dog named Charlie and a parrot named Polly.

Houdini and Bess continued to enjoy each other's company, although some of Houdini's diary entries reflect that he treated her at times more like a griping mother than like a wife. He also made it clear to her that his devotion would have to be shared with his mother, and then the memory of his mother when Cecilia passed away. Houdini obsessed about another man benefiting from his hard work and savings. He repeatedly made Bess promise that if she should remarry after he died, that she insist that her second husband sign a prenuptial agreement agreeing to not pursue any part of Bess's estate that came out of her marriage to Houdini. Houdini took out a large life insurance policy naming Bess as his beneficiary and put the Harlem brownstone in her name.

As many opportunities as Houdini must have had to cheat on Bess, there is only evidence of one affair: with the widow of his famous friend Jack London, Charmian London. In 1918, after Jack had passed away, Charmian spent a winter in New York City. Houdini invited her to come see his show "Cheer Up" in January, and diary entries on her part reflect that soon thereafter he and she started a love affair. Houdini's own records reflect that he felt troubled by his infidelity, and the physical aspect of their affair seems to have died out relatively quickly, even before Charmian returned to California. Houdini and Charmian continued to exchange amorous letters, however. It is unclear if Bess ever knew of the affair; she did speak of discovering love letters from several women to her husband after Houdini's death, one of which she said came from a widow whom she had trusted, possibly Charmian. Bess also complained when Houdini played the lover of younger female actresses during his film career. Charmian and Houdini met up again in 1924 when

Houdini was performing in California, but there is no evidence that their love affair continued at that time.

Normally Houdini and Bess made an event out of their anniversary; for several years they took trips out to Coney Island in New York City, the site of their honeymoon. For their twenty-fifth anniversary, in June of 1919, Houdini threw an elaborate banquet at a Los Angeles hotel (the pair was living in Los Angeles at the time in order to accommodate Houdini's acting career, see Chapter VIX). Two hundred guests attended and gourmet food was served. The couple made an entrance and Bess reportedly nearly fainted. A letter from Houdini from that night reflects his genuine affection for Bess and for the life they had built together. From their thirtieth anniversary, in 1924, there remains a photo of them tied together, kissing.

Family Life

Houdini's devotion to his mother Cecilia is extensively documented; he regarded her as a saint and took great pride in providing for her as his father had asked him to do on his deathbed. Houdini lavished gifts on Cecilia and moved her into 278. Biographers speculate that Houdini viewed Cecilia as one of the only people in his life that was entirely loyal to him, and with whom he did not have to compete with anyone to earn love and acceptance. In return, he worshipped her and craved her happiness. A famous picture of Houdini shows him posing between Cecilia and his wife Bess, eyebrows raised, very content with position between what he called the two women in his life.

In July of 1913, Houdini set sail for a tour in Europe. His mother and some other family members came to the dock as usual to see him off, and Houdini made a big show of running off the boat several times to give his mother another last kiss. His mother said to him, as she always did before he left on a big trip, that perhaps she wouldn't be there when he got back. Houdini tried to cheer her up, and she told him to get her some slippers. Shortly thereafter, Cecilia suffered a stroke from which she would not recover. Houdini received the news that she was gravely ill and hurried back to the States, but too late: Cecilia died on July 17, 1913. Houdini begged the family to postpone the funeral, which they defied Jewish tradition to do. Houdini finally arrived in New York and sat with his mother's body all night.

At the age of thirty-nine, Houdini suffered the loss of his mother with great despair. He returned to performing but continued to have spells of loneliness and grief over Cecilia's death. Houdini also missed his father, attending rabbinical services every year on the anniversary of Meyer's death. He visited his mother Cecilia's grave often and on all anniversaries of her death and his birthday. He even had Cecilia's mother unburied from her grave and buried next to Cecilia. He arranged for a huge monument known as an exedra to be placed on his family plot, which he dedicated on October 1, 1916, even though large gravesite monuments are frowned upon in the Jewish cultural tradition.

After his mother's death, Houdini rented out the old Harlem brownstone and stayed with his brother Dash (Hardeen) and Dash's wife Elsie. Houdini had always maintained a close relationship with Dash, who seemed content to give him center stage. Dash suffered from ulcers and other stomach problems. He and his wife had two children. Houdini also had a loving if distant relationship with his younger sister Gladys, who suffered from health problems that left her at least partially blind. Originally proud of his brother Leo, a young doctor who had a reputation for womanizing, Houdini turned against his brother when Leo married the ex-wife of their other brother Nat, strongly suggesting that there had been an affair during the marriage. Houdini considered this a huge scandal.

Houdini's letters also reflect some tension between himself and Dash and his wife while the families cohabitated. In

February of 1918, Houdini and Bess moved back into the Harlem brownstone where his mother had spent her last days. In his early fifties, Houdini wrote his will, going to great lengths to make sure that the sister-in-law who had divorced one brother and married another would not get any share of his riches, nor would the second brother she had married. Houdini's brother Bill died in 1925 of tuberculosis, an illness he had fought most of his life.

In 1905 Bess, recovering from a serious illness, told Houdini she wanted her mother. Bess's mother, a Catholic, had disowned her eighteen-year-old daughter twelve years earlier when she married the Jewish Houdini. Houdini went to his mother-in-law's apartment and reportedly refused to leave until Mrs. Rahner came with him to 278 to see Bess. Apparently Bess's mother accepted, and she and Bess immediately began crying upon seeing each other. Bess was then thirty years old. The two reconciled, and Mrs. Rahner resolved to accept Houdini as her son-in-law. She seemed to do so with some success, although some reports maintained that she sprinkled holy water about the house after Houdini's visits. Later on in life she moved into 278 and accepted Houdini's financial support.

VIII. Houdini, the Writer

Read It and Know It

After reading this chapter, you will know more about

- **An educational insecurity:** An impoverished background deprived Houdini of a formal education, and he strived to make up for the lack.
- **The first popular book:** Houdini's first major book caused controversy in the world of magicians.
- **More controversy:** Additional books made both law enforcement and the public unhappy with Houdini.
- **Houdini's ghostwriters:** Many of the magician's books were not his own words.

While touring in Europe, Houdini attempted to join the literary world, writing articles for magic and theatrical publications. His biographers suggest that editors really did most of the work on these journalistic pieces, as Houdini in truth had poor grammar and did not type very clearly due to his lack of formal education. Houdini nevertheless set his sights on writing a book documenting the history of magicians. He was determined to gain a reputation an educated, intelligent man and not be known merely as an entertainer.

After his return to the United States, Houdini published some short stories and a ninety-six page book exposing fraudulent magicians and conmen, called *The Right Way to Do Wrong*. Biographers strongly suggest that another writer largely wrote this piece as well. Houdini also published a monthly magazine known as *Conjurers' Monthly*. In *Conjurers' Monthly*, he fought openly and publically with other magicians and writers, especially competing and sparring with another magic magazine, *the Sphinx*, published by a Dr. Wilson. The refusal of the Society of Magicians (or SAM) to adopt *Conjurers' Monthly* as its official magazine led to Houdini's resignation from that organization, although he later rejoined and became president.

In his first major book, *The Unmasking of Robert-Houdin*, Houdini attempted to discredit every claim to fame made by his former hero, Robert-Houdin, explaining how each contribution attributed to Robert-Houdin could be traced back to earlier artists. The passion with which he attacked Robert-Houdin caused controversy in the magicians' community, as Houdini allowed Robert-Houdin almost no credit for any work. His contempt for all imitators seemed to be focused on his former idol, and Houdini's own obsession with being the first and the best seemed to blind him to some historical realities. For his part, Houdini believed the book provided a service to all who had been robbed by Robert-Houdin of the fame that they deserved.

Around 1910, after Houdini announced that he would no longer do handcuff tricks, he wrote a book called *Handcuff Secrets*. This book worried law enforcement officials around the world, who thought of it as a guide for criminals on how to open locks and escape cells.

Continuing his literary endeavors, Houdini wrote a second edition of *The Unmasking of Robert-Houdin*, and co-wrote a book called *History Makers in the World of Magic*. In 1918 and 1919, Houdini wrote a column called M-U-M (Magic – Unity – Might) for the Society of American Magicians' magazine. He also wrote many other articles and participated in the publication of several other books about magic, although it seems likely that he hired others and used Oscar Teale to do the bulk of the research and writing on these numerous pieces (see Chapter XII for more information about Oscar Teale).

In the early 1920s Houdini published the book *Miracle Mongers and their Methods*. Most biographers acknowledge that this book was really ghostwritten, even though it does draw heavily on Houdini's many experiences during his early career in vaudeville and circus performance.

Houdini's crusade to expose fraudulent mediums led to his publication of another work of significant length, a book called *A Magician Among the Spirits*. This book was organized around exposures of famous mediums from history, and chapters explaining the various phenomena produced by "physical" mediums—those who produced physical effects such as the movement of objects, the production of ectoplasm, and the writing or drawing of words and pictures rather than who proclaimed to have psychic powers. Although Houdini prided himself on producing a work of historical accuracy and scientific significance, in reality *A Magician Among the Spirits*, although well received, contained a number of errors and plenty of personal biases, including a rant against Sir Arthur

Conan Doyle (see Chapter XI). It is also a matter of debate how much of the work Houdini produced himself and how much he farmed out to ghostwriters.

In the early 1920s, some combination of Houdini and his ghostwriters authored a romantic detective novel called *The Zanetti Mystery*. Houdini also claimed to have authored short stories for the publication *Weird Tales*, which were supposedly autobiographical. In reality, the stories were based on Houdini's incredible imaginations of escapes from burials inside ancient pyramids and gothic dungeons and were written by the later famous author H.P. Lovecraft. Another controversial claim to literary fame by Houdini arose in 1923, when he claimed to have edited the long-awaited biography of a revered deceased magician named James Elliott, who was famous for his card tricks. Another magician, Clinton Burgess, disputed Houdini's editorship, insisting that he was the editor and Houdini merely provided funding for the book's publication. Burgess and Houdini fought publically and bitterly, and Houdini succeeded in getting Burgess kicked out of the SAM, although it is debatable how much editing Houdini actually did and how much he again turned over to Teale and to other contractors.

Houdini continued to write up to his death. During the summer of 1926, he worked on a book about superstition and wrote an article on masonry and occultism.

In Houdini's Words

Houdini was, as is mentioned above, eager to establish himself as a scholar despite his lack of formal education. In *The Unmasking of Robert-Houdin*, the lengthy defense of his methods hints at this insecurity.

The true historian does not compile. He delves for facts and proofs, and having found these he arrays his indisputable facts, his uncontrovertible proofs, to refute the statements of those who have merely compiled. That is what I have done to prove my case against Robert-Houdin. I have not borrowed from the books of other writers on magic. I have gone to the very fountain head of information, records of contemporary literature, newspapers, programmes and advertisements of magicians who preceded Robert-Houdin, sometimes by a century. It would cost fully a million dollars to forge the collection of evidence now in my hands. Men who lived a hundred years before Robert-Houdin was born did not invent posters or write advertisements in order to refute the claims of those who were to follow in the profession of magic. These programmes, advertisements, newspaper notices, and crude cuts trace the true history of magic as no romancer, no historian of a single generation possibly could. They are the ghosts of dead and gone magicians, rising in this century of research and progress to claim the credit due them.

IX. Houdini, the Movie Star and Producer

Read It and Know It

After reading this chapter, you will know more about

- ***Merveilleux Exploits du Celebre Houdini a Paris:*** Houdini's first movie showcased his talents and set him up as a hero.
- **The failed entrepreneur:** Houdini, wanting to capitalize on the Hollywood craze, started a production company that did not do well.
- **Tricks revealed:** Houdini allowed some of his secrets to be shown on the silver screen.
- **More lawsuits:** The litigious nature of the magician made for a bumpy road in Hollywood.
- **The end of the era:** As with flying, Houdini's stint in film was relatively short-lived.

Houdini was fascinated by film both because of his desire to stay current with the changing times and because he saw the opportunity to immortalize his talents. His first foray into acting came in a brief movie he made in Paris called *Merveilleux Exploits du Celebre Houdini a Paris.* In the film, Houdini shows himself defending a drunk from police brutality, only to be arrested and placed in a cell with a straitjacket. Fortunately, the King of Handcuffs cannot be restrained by such trivialities, and quickly escapes the straitjacket and the handcuffs the cops clap on him, and soon after, a locked cell. No complete version of this movie survives.

Houdini's second appearance on film is no less dramatic or self-focused. While debuting his incredibly dangerous Manacled Bridge Jump in Rochester, New York, he had himself filmed. The film shows Houdini diving from a high bridge into the river below and coming up out of the water miraculously free of handcuffs.

By 1915 motion pictures threatened to end the careers of vaudeville performers worldwide. Houdini, determined as always to stay relevant, turned his attention more fully to entering into the world of film. He served as a consultant for the special effects of a horror movie. He signed a contract to play *Twenty Thousand Leagues Under the Sea's* Captain Nemo, but the film died in production. As resilient as ever, Houdini jumped into the film industry by starting a production company, the Film Development Company (FDC), which performed automatic film processing.

In the summer of 1918, Houdini began filming a series called *"The Master Mystery."* The series was a total of fifteen episodes, each of which featured Houdini escaping from a new, terrifying predicament. The public can see slightly more of how Houdini does his tricks on film than they had been allowed to see during Houdini's live performances. In one film Houdini is seen picking a lock with a piece of an umbrella and some string. In another they see him using his toes as if they were fingers. In January of 1919, the serial was released, and although it aired in many countries, reviewers didn't think much of Houdini as an actor, describing him as having very little range. His escapes, however, were praised as thrilling, even though the audience had no way to know if Houdini was actually performing them or if film manipulation was merely making it seem so. Houdini ran into legal problems collecting his share of the serial's profits, however, and eventually fought and won a four-year battle in court against the company that produced the movie.

By late 1918, Houdini's company the FDC had begun experiencing serious financial trouble. Houdini was especially worried about this business's failure because he had involved friends and family; his brother Dash had left his performing career to manage the company full time, and his friend and mentor Keller had purchased many shares.

In spring of 1919, Houdini and Bess moved from New York to Los Angeles in order to star in a serial called *The Grim Game*. The film again depicted Houdini escaping from unbelievably life-threatening situations. During the filming, an actual, unplanned plane crash is filmed, although Houdini wasn't actually in any danger during the crash, as his "midair stunt" was filmed on the ground. The film was well received as a thriller, and Houdini was signed to another movie called *Terror Island*. Most of that movie was shot on California's wild Catalina Island. The film's gimmicky presentation caused contempt from reviewers, although Houdini was as usual quite pleased with it.

At the end of 1919, Houdini departed the United States for Europe, intending to work on his film career. *The Master Mystery* had been a hit in England, and Houdini earned huge salaries performing there, although some audiences complained that they wanted Houdini to spend more time performing tricks and less time speaking about his film career and other endeavors. Houdini decided to produce his own movies, in which he would of course star. He shot scenes for a movie about counterfeiting that he intended to make.

In the summer of 1920 Houdini returned to the U.S. He devoted himself entirely to his movies, not performing onstage at all for the next year and a half. During this time, Houdini produced and starred in a movie called *The Man from Beyond*. The plot centers on a character who is revived after having been frozen in ice for one hundred years. The man, whose initials are HH like Harry Houdini's, recognizes that a woman about to be married to another man is a descendant of his former fiancée and performs many death-defying stunts to win her over and escape enemies of their union. The movie contains Spiritualistic elements, and it is unclear in the movie if Houdini is receptive to the religion, or if he is just using its wild popularity to score viewers. Houdini certainly worked very hard to publicize the film; he formed four touring companies to promote the film and toured himself to promote it.

Meanwhile, the financial troubles of Houdini's company, the FDC, deepened. In desperation, Houdini started a second company to support the FDC, the Weehawken Street Corporation, which dealt in real estate. However, that company did not prosper, and when the FDC was sued, became a serious financial liability.

Houdini's last film, *Haldane of the Secret Service*, featuring another main character with the initials HH, came out in 1923 to poor reviews. The movie as usual starred Houdini, this time as a secret service agent for the United States who performs incredible stunts.

By the early 1920s, Houdini's film career was over, although Houdini was still involved in many lawsuits stemming from various contracts and corporations associated with his ventures in film. In some cases, Houdini was the plaintiff and in some, the defendant.

X. Houdini, the Collector

Read It and Know It

After reading this chapter, you will know more about

- **Houdini's collection:** Any item that related to magic interested Houdini.
- **Collecting and continued insecurities:** Houdini included drama and literature in his collection to help fulfill his desire to be considered well educated.
- **Alfred Becks:** Houdini hired a full-time librarian to handle his large collection.
- **The collection today:** The magic library is in the hands of the Library of Congress.

Beginning in his youth, Houdini passionately collected books, artifacts, and historical memorabilia related to magic. An old man named Evanion approached Houdini during one of Houdini's first tours of London. Evanion, although a man of modest means, was a collector of rare artifacts from the history of magic. Houdini became an admirer of Evanion's collection and bought several items from him. He treated Evanion fondly and wrote sadly about his passing. Houdini hauled his massive magic library around with him, eventually establishing a huge collection in his home in New York. The library included a great deal of literature on the topic of Spiritualism.

With his determination to become a film star and his eternal desire to prove himself a learned and cultured man, Houdini also became obsessed with accumulating a library of drama and theater literature and memorabilia. He reached out to Robert Gould Shaw, a famous drama collector affiliated with Harvard University, and George Pierce Baker, the creator of the Yale School of Drama. In October of 1919, Houdini's drama collection received a huge infusion when he sent an agent to a large drama sale at the American Art Galleries in New York. His Harlem brownstone was flooded with thousands more programs, playbills, and other items from his purchases. The upstairs floors were so stuffed with Houdini's collections of dramatic literature and magic memorabilia that he had to hire a full-time librarian to organize it in the early 1920s. The librarian, Alfred Becks, had formerly worked for Robert Gould Shaw at the Harvard drama library. Becks lived at the brownstone for a year and a half, working full-time on Houdini's collections. Houdini, however, acknowledged that he was behind the game in the collection of theater literature and that his collection of magic literature was his crowning achievement.

Houdini's dedication to developing a library chronicling the history of magic paid off; he developed a huge library including books, playbills, and other artifacts from the history of magic, which is now housed at the Library of

Congress. He also briefly attempted to bring to life a theater devoted exclusively to magic. In July of 1919, Houdini purchased the oldest magic shop in the United States, Martinka & Company. As president and majority stockholder of the New York business, Houdini opened "Martinka's Magical Place" in the Bronx. However, by the time six months had passed, Houdini had already sold his shares in Martinka & Co, and his theatre idea with it.

In his early fifties, Houdini bragged to friends that he spent only five months a year working, and the rest of his time in his library. He continued to add to both his drama and his magic library, insuring it for a great sum of money. His longtime librarian, Alfred Becks, died in 1925 at the age of eighty. Houdini mourned his passing both for its toll on his collections and for the loss of his friend. In his will, made out in 1925, Houdini left his magic library to the Library of Congress, where it is today, and his drama library to Bess.

In Houdini's Words

Houdini's relationship with Evanion was an important one to the magician, both for its own sake and for the access it gave him to the history of magic. In *The Unmasking of Robert-Houdin*, Houdini remembers his relationship with Evanion.

Often when the bookshops and auction sales did not yield fruit worth plucking, I had the good fortune to meet a private collector or a retired performer whose assistance proved invaluable, and the histories of these meetings read almost like romances, so skilfully did the Fates seem to juggle with my efforts to secure credible proof.

To the late Henry Evans Evanion I am indebted for many of the most important additions to my collection of conjuring curios and my library of magic, recognized by fellow-artistes and litterateurs as the most complete in the world.

Evanion was an Englishman, by profession a parlor magician, by choice and habit a collector and savant. He was an entertainer from 1849 to the year of his death. For fifty years he spent every spare hour at the British Museum collecting data bearing on his marvellous collection, and his interest in the history of magic was shared by his excellent wife who conducted a "sweet shop" near one of London's public schools.

While playing at the London Hippodrome in 1904 I was confined to my room by orders of my physician. During this illness I was interviewed by a reporter who, noticing the clippings and bills with which my room was strewn, made some reference to my collection in the course of his article. The very day on which this interview appeared, I received from Henry Evanion a mere scrawl stating that he, too, collected programmes, bills, etc., in which I might be interested.

I wrote at once asking him to call at one o'clock the next afternoon, but as the hour passed and he did not appear, I decided that, like many others who asked for interviews, he had felt but a passing whim. That afternoon about four o'clock my physician suggested that, as the day was mild, I walk once around the block. As I stepped from the lift, the hotel porter informed me that since one o'clock an old man had been waiting to see me, but so shabby was his appearance, they had not dared send him up to my room. He pointed to a bent figure, clad in rusty raiment. When I approached the old man he rose and informed me that he had brought some clippings, bills, etc., for me to see. I asked him to be as expeditious as possible, for I was too weak to stand long and my head was a-whirl from the effects of la grippe.

With some hesitancy of speech but the loving touch of a collector he opened his parcel.

"I have brought you, sir, only a few of my treasures, sir, but if you will call—"
I heard no more. I remember only raising my hands before my eyes, as if I had been dazzled by a sudden shower of diamonds. In his trembling hands lay priceless treasures for which I had sought in vain—original programmes and bills of Robert-Houdin, Phillippe, Anderson, Breslaw, Pinetti, Katterfelto, Boaz, in fact all the conjuring celebrities of the eighteenth century, together with lithographs long considered unobtainable, and newspapers to be found only in the files of national libraries. I felt as if the King of England stood before me and I must do him homage.

Physician or no physician, I made an engagement with him for the next morning, when I was bundled into a cab and went as fast as the driver could urge his horse to Evanion's home, a musty room in the basement of No. 12 Methley Street, Kennington Park Road, S.E.

In the presence of his collection I lost all track of time. Occasionally we paused in our work to drink tea which he made for us on his pathetically small stove. The drops of the first tea which we drank together can yet be found on certain papers in my collection. His wife, a most sympathetic soul, did not offer to disturb us, and it was 3:30 the next morning, or very nearly twenty-four hours after my arrival at his home, when my brother, Theodore Weiss (Hardeen), and a thoroughly disgusted physician appeared on the scene and dragged me, an unwilling victim, back to my hotel and medical care.

Such was the beginning of my friendship with Evanion. In time I learned that some of his collection had been left to him by James Savren, an English barber, who was so interested in magic that at frequent intervals he dropped his trade to work without pay for famous magicians, including Döbler, Anderson, Compars Herrmann, De Liska, Wellington Young, Cornillot, and Gyngell. From these men he had secured a marvellous collection, which was the envy of his friendly rival, Evanion. Savren bequeathed his collection to Evanion, and bit by bit I bought it from the latter, now poverty stricken, too old to work and physically failing. These purchases I made at intervals whenever I played in London, and on June 7th, 1905, while playing at Wigan, I received word that Evanion was dying at Lambeth Infirmary.

After the show, I jumped to London, only to find that cancer of the throat made it almost impossible for him to speak intelligibly. I soon discovered, however, that his chief anxiety was for the future of his wife and then for his own decent burial. When these sad offices had been provided for, he became more peaceful, and when I rose to leave him, knowing that we had met probably for the last time, he drew forth his chiefest treasure, a superb book of Robert-Houdin's programmes, his one legacy, which is now the central jewel in my collection. Evanion died ten days later,

June 17th, and within a short time his good wife followed him into the Great Unknown.

XI. Houdini, the Crusader against Spiritualism

Read It and Know It

After reading this chapter, you will know more about

- **Sir Arthur Conan Doyle:** The creator of Sherlock Holmes was a devout believer in Spiritualism.
- ***A Magician Among the Spirits:*** Houdini's book sought to expose fraudulent mediums.
- **Mina "Margery" Crandon:** Houdini eventually exposed the famous Boston medium after a long and public struggle.
- **Robert Gysel and Rose Mackenberg:** These informants joined Houdini in his campaign to debunk Spiritualism.

Spiritualism, a religion and movement born in the late eighteenth century, became very trendy after World War I. Spiritualists believed that the spirits of the dead could communicate with the living through mediums. They did so during séances, in which a group of "sitters" came and sat in front of a medium, holding hands in a darkened room while the medium summoned the spirits of the dead.

Houdini had in the past scorned Spiritualism as fraudulent and manipulative of mourning individuals who had lost loved ones. At the same time, the loss of his mother left him yearning for the ability to reach her somehow. Whatever his real beliefs, he made a pact with Bess and several other friends to speak a certain word if summoned by a medium after death, in order to have final proof on the matter. Further, even at the height of his crusade against Spiritualism, he never claimed to attack the tenets of the religion itself; rather, he set out to expose fraud on the part of persons who claimed to be mediums.

The worlds of magic and Spiritualism overlapped both practically and culturally; the popularity of Spiritualism ignited the public's interest in magic, and further, magicians and mediums used similar techniques to perform their arts. Houdini's fame as a magician and manic drive to expose all that threatened his trade put him on an inevitable crash course with the religion. The collision was played out in part through his friendship with the author Sir Arthur Conan Doyle.

Houdini and Sir Arthur Conan Doyle

Sir Arthur Conan Doyle, most renowned for his authorship of the Sherlock Holmes mysteries, was also an evangelical Spiritualist in his later days after having lost his son in Word War I. Well-known as a writer, Doyle was originally an eye doctor and belonged to a scholarly level of society that Houdini often seemed to ache to join. In addition, Doyle fit the role of an ideal man of the time; he was tall, muscular, athletic, wealthy, and cultured. He and Houdini shared a passion for the sport of boxing. When Houdini traveled to Europe in 1920, he mailed Doyle a copy of his book, *The Unmasking of Robert-Houdin*. Doyle read it and wanted to discuss Houdini's representation of the famous Davenport Brothers, magicians whom Houdini had met. Doyle believed that the brothers were able to do their escape art because they were mediums, able to de-materialize and reconstitute their physical forms. In his eagerness to make friends with Doyle, Houdini didn't contradict him. In fact, Houdini indicated to Doyle that he was interested in looking into Spiritualism with an open mind. Doyle believed that Houdini himself might be able de-materialize in order to do his tricks.

Doyle sent Houdini to mediums Doyle trusted, one of whom performed the then-popular form of speaking with spirits by manifesting ectoplasm, a gooey substance in the shape of someone or something or that appeared to be a living substance. Houdini failed to be convinced by these demonstrations, recognizing the ways that such tricks could be arranged. However, his desire to be friends with Doyle, whom he found intelligent and fascinating, led him to hold back from being open with Doyle about his doubts. Houdini attended many séances.

Doyle and Houdini's friendship began to fall apart when Doyle came to the United States to promote Spiritualism in 1922. At that time, Doyle was especially passionate about a new trend in Spiritualism called "spirit photography," in which everyday photographs captured a spirit image. Houdini, who knew something about film development from his film company (see Chapter IX), recognized that the "spirit" images could be doctored into the photographs. He even hired a team of investigators to try to find out the methods of famous spirit photographers. Houdini became less enthralled with Doyle as he saw how naïve Doyle was; magicians well known to Houdini, the Zancigs, had convinced Doyle that they were clairvoyants during a private session. Similarly, Houdini tried to explain to Doyle how the spiritualist phenomenon of "spirit hands," or hands that appeared in wax during séances, could be made by humans. Doyle refused to give Houdini's explanations any weight. While in the States, Doyle saw a famous medium named Besinnet, with whom Houdini tried to gain a meeting through Doyle's introduction. However, Besinnet refused to answer Houdini's requests, probably wisely, as Houdini had done some research on her methods and had likely already concluded that she was a fraud.

During the summer of 1922, Houdini and Bess joined Doyle and his family in Atlantic City for a weekend of fun and relaxation. During this visit, Doyle's wife, who claimed to be able to perform "trance-writing," a method of communicating with spirits by which the medium writes messages from the dead, summoned Houdini for a session. In that session, with Doyle present, she produced fifteen pages of writing supposedly from Houdini's mother, Cecilia. While the Doyles thought that Houdini came out of this experience with unmistakable proof of his dead mother's presence and Spiritualism as a whole, Houdini really emerged highly skeptical that his mother was involved with the writing. However, he said nothing of this to the Doyles, wanting to keep the peace.

In October 1922 Houdini got into trouble with both the magician community and the Spiritualists when he published an article explaining a common trick of both, the placement of a radio transmitter inside a non-descript household object to create noises and voices seemingly from magic or spirits. The Society of American Magicians, of which Houdini was president, formed a special committee to make sure that neither Houdini nor other magicians exposed any more of their trade secrets. The SAM also criticized Houdini for writing a monthly column in a New York paper, teaching young readers how to do minor magic tricks. Houdini further clashed with Howard Thurston, his deceased mentor Keller's protégée. Thurston was a believer in Spiritualism and had attended séances with Besinnet. Thurston was also one of the few magicians who came anywhere close to Houdini's skill and fame, the more likely reason for their rivalry.

After Doyle returned to England, Houdini and his friend began to have disagreements by letter about various aspects of Spiritualism. In October of 1922, Houdini published an article in a New York paper essentially stating Houdini's conviction that mediums and séances were fraudulent. Doyle was sent the article by someone, and for the first time the friends argued openly about Spiritualism. Houdini explained how the trance-writing session that he had endured with the Doyles in Atlantic City had left him convinced not of Spiritualism's truth, but of its lack thereof. Doyle answered by explaining away each of the reasons that Houdini had found to disbelieve the truth of the session. Soon, Doyle and Houdini were fighting publically in an exchange of letters published in *The New York Times*. When Doyle returned to the United States for a second tour, the two men met up in Denver, Colorado. Despite efforts to patch their relationship, Houdini agreed to meet with a reporter who had written an article claiming that Doyle had dared him to come to a séance, where he would produce Houdini's mother. This publicity put more strain on the friendship. After Doyle had returned to England, Doyle similarly reacted gullibly to a supposed jab by Houdini in a California newspaper. The two men finally dissolved their friendship.

Houdini, the Lecturer and Investigator

By 1924, Houdini was becoming recognized nationally as an investigator and educator on the subject of fraudulent techniques used by mediums. He toured the United States, giving lectures at universities about the history of Spiritualism and the ways that fraudulent mediums produced their effects. Houdini also "tested" mediums. Most famously, he reproduced the powers of a renowned Spanish medium who called himself Argamasilla, who claimed to be able to see through metal. He also duplicated mediums' use of telepathy, organizing a test at his house in which he went into another room while his guests selected topics at random, returning to the room to explain (correctly) what he had "telepathically received" from them while in the other room. He jokingly performed a "teleportation" of a writer to a benefit held by the Society of American Magicians, pretending that the speaker was communicating via radio, but concealing the man in the banquet hall, who emerged after announcing he was teleporting in for the event. During his push to expose fraud among mediums, Houdini wrote and published a book called *A Magician Among the Spirits*.

The Scientific American Committee

Houdini's most longstanding battle in his fight against fraudulent Spiritualist mediums began in January of 1924, when he was nominated to an investigative committee put together by the magazine *Scientific American*. The purpose of the committee was to determine who, if anyone, would be the winner of two cash prizes offered to the first two individuals who produced a psychic object or photograph while working under the committee's strictly controlled test conditions. The other members of the committee were largely academics and scientists, including two individuals from the Society of Psychical Research (the SPR), a United Kingdom-based nonprofit dedicated to objectively researching paranormal phenomena. J. Malcolm Bird, an editor at *Scientific American*, served as the secretary for the committee.

With his large ego and longstanding need to prove himself as an intellectual, Houdini began clashing with his fellow committee members almost immediately. After the committee had tested a medium named George Valentine and found evidence of fraud, Houdini immediately told the press about the committee's discoveries. Other committee members, especially Bird, objected to Houdini's violation of the bylaw that none of the members speak to the press individually, for fear of discouraging future candidates from coming forward to compete for the prizes.

Due either to Houdini's indiscretion or to some other reason, no other viable medium came forth to try for the prize for six more months, until Nino Pecoraro, a young Italian medium, volunteered. Pecoraro was interesting to the committee because he claimed to be channeling the famous deceased medium Eusapia Palladino. Bird, perhaps intentionally, failed to tell Houdini about the first two test séances that the committee held with Pecoraro. However, by the third, Houdini had caught wind of the tests and arrived to evaluate Pecoraro. During his séances, Pecoraro seemed to make things appear and sounds occur while bound tightly. Houdini showed Pecoraro what it really meant to be bound, tying him intricately and knowledgably from his own years of experience as an escape artist. Bound thusly, Pecoraro was unable to produce the same effects as he had during the first two "tests," proving that he himself, and not a spiritual force, had produced the noises and images in the prior séances.

After Pecoraro, the committee took on the testing of a medium who called herself Margery. Margery's real name was Mina Crandon, and she was the young, well-to-do wife of a surgeon and Harvard professor named Dr. Crandon. The aristocratic pair lived in beautiful four-story house on Beacon Hill in Boston and enjoyed an educated and cultured circle of friends and colleagues. Margery purported to produce messages from the dead in several languages and, most famously, to channel her deceased brother Walter, a young man who had been killed while working on the railroad. Margery had gained a large following of believers who praised her powers as a medium, including Sir Arthur Conan Doyle. Again, Bird failed to tell Houdini about thirty séance tests that were held with Margery in the first half of 1924. Upon discovering that the committee was close to awarding a prize to Margery, Houdini intervened and insisted on evaluating her for himself. Bird, who had been staying with the Crandons, and who Houdini already suspected of aiding the couple in fraud in order to gain their friendship, was forced to agree.

In July of 1924, Houdini and other committee members began a series of séances with Margery in Boston. Houdini quickly detected that Margery used her foot to ring a bell supposedly rung by Walter and that she used her head to move objects while her hands and feet were held by other sitters. Houdini tried to convince the committee to immediately publish his discoveries, but Bird convinced the group to sit with Margery for another series of séances before deciding. Houdini believed, probably correctly, that Margery and Dr. Crandon used their unusually close relationship with Bird to find out what Houdini knew about Margery's methods.

For the second round of séances, held the following month, Houdini convinced a *Scientific American* committee member named Walter Franklin Prince, head of the American Society for Psychical Research, to attend. Houdini and an assistant named Collins built a special cabinet for Margery to sit in. It was designed to prevent her from using her tricks to manipulate a bell and other items. In a very tense series of séances that stretched over two days, Houdini and Margery accused each other of planting various items in the box and in the bell, Houdini insisting that Margery was using a tool to ring the bell from far off and Margery insisting that Houdini was planting tools on her and blocking the bell.

During these two tense days, Bird stepped down as secretary of the committee and Prince took over the post. Margery's spirit brother Walter "cursed out" Houdini, telling him to leave, which amused Houdini, as he knew Walter was not really speaking but one of the Crandons. In earlier séances, Walter had revealed "his" anti-Semitic feelings towards Houdini, a sentiment that Dr. Crandon mirrored in his correspondence with Sir Arthur Conan Doyle. By the last séance of the month, Margery failed to produce any communications or signs from the dead. Houdini triumphantly told the committee that her failure was due to the fact that she was restrained from performing her techniques by the box he and Collins and built and left Boston convinced that she was a fraud.

The committee, never having all sat together at the same time for a séance with Margery, remained divided for a long time about whether to credit Margery with the prize or to denounce her as a fraud. The group polarized between Houdini and a committee member named Carrington, a writer of many articles of psychical research. Houdini insisted that he had already detected that Margery was a fraud and that the public should know about her deception— and his role in discovering it—as soon as possible. Carrington insisted that Margery was genuinely communicating with the spirits. McDougall, a scientist and committee member who had never actually attended any of the séances, took no side but complained to the newspapers that Houdini acted like Houdini was the only one qualified to judge the matter, when he, McDougall, a professor and scientist, knew as much or more than a magician. This, as well as the fact that supporters of Margery publically declaimed Houdini as merely an ignorant magician, infuriated Houdini, who was sensitive as always to being classified as inferior to academics and aristocrats.

When the committee failed to reach a decision after another round of séances with Margery, Houdini traveled to Boston to expose her himself and prove his worth to the world. In January of 1925, Houdini staged a show at Boston's Symphony Hall, inviting Margery to come and perform, and offering her his own prize of ten thousand dollars if she succeeded in escaping detection of fraud. Predictably, Margery did not show up, but Houdini, not to be deterred from exposing her, put on a two-hour show replicating her tricks with some blindfolded sitters, while the audience had full view of how he perpetrated the phenomena. His program included tricks performed from inside supposedly the same cabinet that he had made for Margery, although it was later revealed that the cabinet was probably a replica.

Committee members, including Prince, whom Houdini had trusted as an ally, and McDougall, whom Houdini had made up with after McDougall's insults, reacted by publishing statements disapproving of Houdini's show and asserting that Houdini's replication of Margery's tricks had proved nothing. Doyle joined the fray by publishing an article about his view of Margery's abilities, aimed to discredit Houdini's reputation as a serious investigator of Spiritualism. In addition, the publisher of *Scientific American*, Orson Munn, had become fed up by the way Houdini had changed the magazine's scientific investigation into a Houdini-focused publicity stunt. Public supporters of Margery spread the news that many mediums predicted that Houdini would be dead within a year, a well-deserved punishment for his harassment of one of their revered leaders.

Enraged and betrayed, Houdini held a six-week show at New York's Hippodrome Theater in which he continued to produce phenomena that supposedly only mediums could evoke through channeling spirits, including supposedly predicting two events before they happened (in reality, Houdini had journalist friends give him the information before it went to the press). The Crandons retaliated by holding a lecture in Boston, to which they invited professors from Harvard and the Massachusetts Institute of Technology (MIT) and other academic elites, where they illustrated

Margery's abilities in a slide presentation. A researcher from the Society of Psychical Research named Eric Dingwall, a former magician whom Houdini had considered to be an ally, spoke, devoting considerable time to criticizing Houdini's qualifications to judge Margery's abilities, and recommending that Margery come for further study in England. McDougall chaired the lecture.

The committee's deadlock was finally broken when the Crandons refused to continue to submit to testing unless Houdini was removed from the committee. Munn, the publisher of *Scientific American*, for all that he resented Houdini's showmanship while serving on the committee, refused to remove Houdini, and the Crandons withdrew from the investigation. The committee members then voted four to one that there was no basis for believing that Margery's skills came from supernatural sources. Prince and McDougall released separate, individual statements indicating that they had not been convinced that Margery had any paranormal abilities.

The Crandons attacked the verdict, saying that they had withdrawn from the test, not that the committee who had come to a decision. Houdini, infuriated by the weak language of the verdict, harangued Prince to release the truth to the public—that he, Houdini, had discovered not only a lack of proof of paranormal ability but also that Margery had engaged in several fraudulent tactics. Prince refused and resigned as head of the American Society of Psychical Researchers, exhausted and disgusted by the dramatic fighting. The American Society of Psychical Researchers was taken over by none other than Houdini's original nemesis on the committee, Bird. Houdini immediately resigned from the American Society of Psychical Researchers.

Not one to submit to less than crushing his opponents, Houdini orchestrated the publication of a pamphlet denouncing an unnamed couple that fraudulently called themselves mediums. Shut out of Margery's séances himself, he sent an undercover agent to infiltrate the goings-on and report back to him, continually replicating whatever stunts that Margery produced onstage so that the Crandons knew that he was watching them.

In 1925 Margery was discredited publically when she was studied by Harvard University's Psychology Department, who discovered and published many of her non-paranormal techniques for producing "communications" from the dead. Houdini was beyond gratified when Walter Franklin Pierce, the committee member who had betrayed him, publically told the papers that he had been wrong and that Houdini had been right. Prince and Houdini re-established their friendship via mail. Houdini was even more thrilled by the timing of the Harvard report, as it gave him the opportunity to humiliate his old enemy J. Malcolm Bird, who had in the meantime published a book devoted to exalting Margery and disparaging Houdini. In 1926 Houdini showed up at a public address of Bird's at a Spiritualist church in Philadelphia and traded bitter speeches with Bird about poor character and deceitful tactics.

Ironically, Houdini later learned from his Boston informant that Margery, who was now reduced back to Mina Crandon and who was drinking herself to death, admired Houdini's ability to see through her act and his determination to stand his ground.

Houdini's Anti-Spiritualist Campaign

After the committee's verdict, Houdini became more aggressive in his efforts to discredit mediums. Not only did Houdini disagree with opportunistically tricking vulnerable and uneducated people out of money, he also espoused the popular theory of the time that Spiritualism could lead people to become insane and/or to commit crimes and pointed out that sexual assaults on women happened under the cover of the séance proceedings.

Houdini essentially opened his own anti-fraud, anti-Spiritualist police force. He advertised in papers that anyone who had been robbed by a medium could write to him for help. He trained the New York Police on tricks used during séances. He also hired his own undercover investigators. Houdini still attended séances and exposed mediums on the spot, often testifying against them later in courts of law. He retained open the $10,000 reward that he had held out to Margery, offering it to any medium who could perform an act that he himself could not duplicate. Mediums who attended his shows were likely to be called out, challenged, and then booed out of the theater, sometimes in tense situations that threatened rioting and violence.

Two of Houdini's most useful informants were Robert Gysel and Rose Mackenberg. Gysel was a magician who lived and performed in the Midwestern states. Gysel used extreme measures to expose mediums, including harassment and prosecution. Mackenberg was a young, non-descript Jewish woman from Brooklyn who traveled around to mediums under various identities, receiving advice and predictions about nonexistent children and husbands. She reported back in writing to Houdini what she learned.

Houdini used Mackenberg to publically humiliate a reverend of the Spiritualist faith, Charles Gunsolas from Indianapolis, who had written to Houdini with a veiled threat that Gunsolas could reveal all of Houdini's methods of doing tricks if Gunsolas wanted to. Houdini sent Mackenberg for some readings with a fictional story of having lost an infant, and Gunsolas provided his medium services to her. When Gunsolas showed up at Houdini's show in Indianapolis, Houdini called him up on the stage and revealed his detective work and the evidence that he had of Gunsolas' fraud.

Houdini scoffed at Spiritualists who called themselves ministers and reverends, pointing out that ministers of other faiths had to undergo years of intensive training, whereas all one had to do to be a Spiritualist leader was to claim psychic powers. To prove his point, Houdini had Mackenberg travel the United States becoming ordained as a Spiritualist minister many times over. Houdini also sent Mackenberg to Massachusetts to purchase the charter of a Spiritualist church, which she was able to do with ease, although Houdini was later court-ordered to return the charter.

Houdini became a hated name among Spiritualists, who attempted to organize themselves to stop his crusade. During his Chicago run of HOUDINI, Houdini and his agents claimed to have exposed nearly eighty cases of medium fraud in the Chicago area. Several mediums brought lawsuits against Houdini for slander and libel, with the amount Houdini was sued for totaling almost a million dollars between the many plaintiffs.

In the mid-1920s, Houdini took his activism against Spiritualism to Congress. A U.S. representative from New York had sponsored a bill banning fortune telling in the District of Columbia. Houdini arrived in Washington, D.C. to testify for four days of hearings in front of the House of Representatives and the Senate. As usual, where Houdini went, drama and entertainment followed. The hearings were packed with angry Spiritualists who booed and heckled Houdini, calling him a liar and a fake. Houdini, as always thriving on attention, took center-stage to cross-examine witnesses, warning mediums that he would find them out and presenting testimony from his investigators, including Mackenberg. An especially juicy scandal erupted when Mackenberg testified that a medium had told her that many members of Congress and the President and his family themselves practiced Spiritualism, provoking the White House to print a denial of these claims. In the long run, the proposed bill did not pass because it violated First Amendment guarantees to freedom of speech and religion. For the first time, perhaps, Houdini reflected that his efforts might have been more effective if he hadn't made the hearings into a one-man Houdini show, thus distracting Congress from the work of passing a bill.

In Houdini's Words

Houdini's book *Miracle Mongers and Their Methods* is dedicated to discussing the kinds of fraudulent mediums Houdini seemed to despise. The first chapters discuss the "fire eaters" of bygone days, and his summary of them not only reveals his contempt for the Spiritualists of his own time, but something of his intimate understanding of how performers depend on trends.

The great day of the Fire-eater—or, should I say, the day of the great Fire-eater—has passed. No longer does fashion flock to his doors, nor science study his wonders, and he must now seek a following in the gaping loiterers of the circus side-show, the pumpkin-and-prize-pig country fair, or the tawdry booth at Coney Island. The credulous, wonder-loving scientist, however, still abides with us and, while his serious-minded brothers are wringing from Nature her jealously guarded secrets, the knowledge of which benefits all mankind, he gravely follows that perennial Will-of-the-wisp, spiritism, and lays the flattering unction to his soul that he is investigating "psychic phenomena," when in reality he is merely gazing with unseeing eyes on the flimsy juggling of pseudo-mediums.

XII. Houdini, the Developer and the Patriot

Read It and Know It

After reading this chapter, you will know more about

- **Houdini and London:** He was founder and president of the London's Magician's club
- **Houdini and SAM:** He had a difficult on/off relationship with the Society of American Magicians.
- **Houdini and the draft:** Despite his age, the magician tried to enlist.
- **Patriotic efforts:** Not to be discouraged by his ineligibility to fight, Houdini tried to help by teaching his tricks to the armed forces.

Houdini and the Clubs

Although Houdini's self-obsession was well known and widely evident, Houdini also made undeniable contributions to the development of magic. In his own career, he demonstrated a huge range of skill and ability to innovate, successfully mastering acts encompassing card tricks, needle swallowing, torturous escapes, and breathtaking illusions. He also worked to organize magicians into a respectable and united force and used his abilities to contribute to charity, safety initiatives, and patriotic works.

While touring in England, Houdini worked to establish an institution for magicians. Always at home in England, he forged a society that dedicated itself to promoting the art of magic and to supporting developing magicians. In 1913 he started the London Magician's Club, which he led as the president.

Back in the U.S., the Society of American Magicians (the SAM) had already been created. Houdini had had a rocky relationship with the SAM due to the competition between his magazine *Conjurers' Monthly* and another SAM members' magazine *The Sphinx*. Houdini had in fact resigned in 1908 from the SAM over this conflict, but in 1912 he was made an honorary member in recognition for his contributions to magic. Although the SAM had been founded in 1902, it had failed to thrive as an organization.

Around 1916 Houdini turned his energies to revitalizing the SAM. He collaborated with Oscar Teale, a retired magician and Columbia University professor, to reach out to local magicians' clubs around the country. Houdini organized, hosted, and paid for dinners for members of these clubs in various cities around the United States, using this platform to speak to the clubs about the importance of joining a larger union. Many clubs did join, the first being the Buffalo Magician's Club from Buffalo, New York. Houdini's contribution to uniting these groups was profound and long lasting; the SAM survives today, with more than 250 member clubs. In 1917 Houdini was elected the SAM's president, which he took on with typical energy. He facilitated meetings of the group, oversaw publication of its monthly magazine, and threw huge banquets for members. He also tried to unite the re-energized SAM with the London Magicians' Club.

Houdini also went out of his way to interview legendary magicians and learn from them. In 1910 Houdini met with the surviving member of the famous magician-spiritualist duo the Davenport Brothers, who showed Houdini some of the Brothers' long-held secrets for doing rope tricks. Houdini also sought out famous German magician Wiljalba Frikell and the family of Robert-Houdin, although he later worked to expose Robert-Houdin as a fraud. Houdini also joined another organization influential to the reputation of magic; in 1923, he became a member of Grand Lodge of the Free and Accepted Masons, and was initiated at St. Cecile's Lodge in New York City. He remained active in the Masons until his death in 1926.

Houdini the Patriot

With the entry of the United States into World War I in 1917, Houdini downplayed his connections with Germany and signed up for the draft. Already forty-three years old, he was not drafted. Houdini instead plunged into efforts to support American troops and their families. He led an initiative for SAM members to perform at army camps. Houdini himself staged performances at large military bases such as Fort Dix and Slocum, and also performed for benefits held by the Red Cross. When the American ship *the Antilles* was sunk, Houdini organized an elaborate benefit for the families of the troops killed on the ship. He recruited SAM magicians to come to the benefit, creating a huge "Carnival of Magic." His crowning achievement, however, was convincing retired magician Heinrich Keller (also known as Harry Kellar) to return to the stage after having been in retirement for ten years. Keller was perhaps the first American-born magician and the only magician that Houdini ever came close to acknowledging as his superior. Keller's re-appearance brought down the house, surpassing even Houdini's performance of the Water Torture Cell.

As the war got into full swing in 1918, Houdini arranged with the Secretary of War to teach American recruits how to escape from sinking vessels and German handcuffs, and how to survive for longer underwater. The practical value of these lessons was probably minimal, but Houdini felt proud of his contributions to the war effort. Further, this is probably one of the only instances in which Houdini volunteered to share with any other person his secret escape techniques, reflecting a real desire to help the American effort.

For six months in 1918, Houdini performed twice a day in a patriotic show called "Cheer Up" at the Hippodrome Theater in New York City. "Cheer Up" featured re-enactments of famous American historical moments and figures and music by John Philip Sousa. During "Cheer Up," Houdini performed the Vanishing Elephant Trick and a form of his Underwater Box Escape. He also continued to give performances at military compounds. He created a group known as the Rabbis' Sons Theatrical Benevolent Association, which raised money for American troops. Houdini was president of the Association.

Houdini also was a major organizer of a major benefit for the wartime hospital fund, and planned to perform a trick in which he seemed to catch a marked bullet fired from a gun. His friend and mentor Keller admonished him not to take on the dangerous trick, which had recently taken the life of a magician friend of Houdini's, and Houdini agreed to do the Upside Down instead. Houdini served as auctioneer of Liberty Bonds at this benefit, bringing in tens of thousands of dollars for the war effort. In the 1920s, Houdini continued his charity work, giving shows to benefit the United Jewish Campaign and performing in children's hospitals and prisons.

After the war, Houdini offered to teach leaders in the U.S. Bureau of Mines how to preserve air in case of mine collapse emergencies. After Houdini managed to stay underwater in an airtight casket in a New York swimming pool in 1926, Dr. W. J. McConnell of the Bureau tried to spread Houdini's lessons outside of the Bureau as well, although most experts did not accept his offer, either not believing that Houdini was authentic or not wanting to be associated with a magician. Houdini also designed a diving suit that he believed would save the lives of divers because it allowed them to exit the suit quickly in case of emergency.

In Houdini's Words

Houdini was not alone in thinking that magic tricks could help humankind. In *Miracle Mongers and Their Methods* he describes how the discoveries of "fire eaters" and their ilk have helped develop tools for modern fire fighting. Houdini's clear pride in the use of magic tricks to save lives comes through in his extensive use of "scientific" evidence.

In our own times the art of defending the hands and face, and indeed the whole body, from the action of heated iron and intense fire, has been applied to the nobler purpose of saving human life, and rescuing property from the flames. The revival and the improvement of this art we owe to the benevolence and the ingenuity of the Chevalier Aldini of Milan, who has travelled through all Europe to present this valuable gift to his species. Sir H. Davy had long ago shown that a safety lamp for illuminating mines, containing inflammable air, might be constructed of wire-gauze, alone, which prevented the flame within, however large or intense, from setting fire to the inflammable air without. This valuable property, which has been long in practical use, he ascribed to the conducting and radiating power of the wire-gauze, which carried off the heat of the flame, and deprived it of its power. The Chevalier Aldini conceived the idea of applying the same material, in combination with other badly conducting substances, as a protection against fire. The incombustible pieces of dress which he uses for the body, arms, and legs, are formed out of strong cloth, which has been steeped in a solution of alum, while those for the head, hands, and feet, are made of cloth of asbestos or amianthus. The head dress is a large cap which envelops the whole head down to the neck, having suitable perforations for the eyes, nose, and mouth. The stockings and cap are single, but the gloves are made of double amianthus cloth, to enable the fireman to take into his hand burning or red-hot bodies. The piece of ancient asbestos cloth preserved in the Vatican was formed, we believe, by mixing the asbestos with other fibrous substances; but M. Aldini has executed a piece of nearly the same size, 9 feet 5 inches long, and 5 feet 3 inches wide, which is much stronger than the ancient piece, and possesses superior qualities, in consequence of having been woven without the introduction of any foreign substance. In this manufacture the fibers are prevented from breaking by action of steam, the cloth is made loose in its fabric, and the threads are about the fiftieth of an inch in diameter.

The metallic dress which is superadded to these means of defence consists of five principal pieces, viz., a casque or cap, with a mask large enough to leave a proper space between it and the asbestos cap; a cuirass with its brassets; a piece of armour for the trunk and thighs; a pair of boots of double wire-gauze; and an oval shield 5 feet long by 2 1/2 feet wide, made by stretching the wire-gauze over a slender frame of iron. All these pieces are made of iron wire-gauze, having the interval between its threads the twenty-fifth part of an inch.

In order to prove the efficacy of this apparatus, and inspire the firemen with confidence in its protection, he showed them that a finger first enveloped in asbestos, and then in a double case of wire-gauze, might be held a long time in the flame of a spirit-lamp or candle before the heat became inconvenient. A fireman having his hand within a double asbestos glove, and its palm protected by a piece of asbestos cloth, seized with impunity a large piece of red hot iron, carried it deliberately to the distance of 150 feet, inflamed straw with it, and brought it back again to the furnace. On other occasions the fireman handled blazing wood and burning substances, and walked during five minutes upon an iron grating placed over flaming fagots.

In order to show how the head, eyes, and lungs are protected, the fireman put on the asbestos and wire-gauze cap, and the cuirass, and held the shield before his breast. A fire of shavings was then lighted, and kept burning in a *large raised chafing-dish; the fireman plunged his head into the middle of the flames with his face to the fuel, and in that position went several times round the chafing-dish for a period longer than a minute. In a subsequent trial, at Paris, a fireman placed his head in the middle of a large brazier filled with flaming hay and wood, and resisted the action of the fire during five or six minutes and even ten minutes.*

In the experiments which were made at Paris in the presence of a committee of the Academy of Sciences, two parallel rows of straw and brushwood supported by iron wires, were formed at the distance of 3 feet from each other, and extended 30 feet in length. When this combustible mass was set on fire, it was necessary to stand at a distance of 8 or 10 yards to avoid the heat. The flames from both the rows seemed to fill up the whole space between them, and rose to the height of 9 or 10 feet. At this moment six firemen, clothed in the incombustible dresses, and marching at a slow pace behind each other, repeatedly passed through the whole length between the two rows of flame, which were constantly fed with additional combustibles. One of the firemen carried on his back a child eight years old, in a wicker-basket covered with metallic gauze, and the child had no other dress than a cap made of amianthine cloth.

XIII. Houdini, the Proud

Read It and Know It

After reading this chapter, you will know more about

- **Houdinize:** The magician was famous enough to inspire a new word.
- **Dash's role:** Houdini set up his brother as a false rival to try to control imitators.
- **The Houdina Company:** Houdini allegedly smashed furniture in a rival's office.
- **Jacob Hyman:** Houdini's old partner claimed a right to the Houdini name.

By his mid-forties, Houdini had surpassed celebrity status and become a living legend. His image and name was known throughout the world, and a dictionary of the time even published an edition with the word "houdinize," meaning to escape or to wriggle out of confinement or restraint. Houdini's legend, however, is not without its detractors. Many magicians in Houdini's time and now have criticized Houdini's massive ego and his willingness to expose other magicians and to stretch the truth in order to stay on top of the magic world.

In the magic community, Houdini was known as a fantastic egomaniac who believed that he was a deity among magicians and conjurers and who loved to talk about himself. Houdini's writing of the Encyclopedia Britannica's entry on "Conjurers" lends support to this opinion, as Houdini spoke only of his own contributions to magic without mentioning a single other magician. Houdini's diary entries also reflect that he got angry when newspapers mentioned lesser magicians than he when he had also performed.

Houdini's fervor to debunk his original icon Robert-Houdin reflects a blinding desire to be known as the best conjurer and mystifier not only of his generation, but also in the history of magic. In fact, Houdini had rocky relationships with most other famous magicians of the time, including Harry Blackstone and Howard Thurston. The only magician that he ever came close to acknowledging might be equal or superior to himself was Heinrich Keller, an American-born magician with whom Houdini formed a close bond.

Houdini's zeal for crushing imitators is also indicative of the size and importance of his ego. While Houdini allowed that other magicians were technically permitted to also do escape tricks, he publically and privately reacted poorly when his imitators used his title, The King of Handcuffs, or the name Houdini. Houdini put ads in newspapers and magic magazines in England and the United States, warning that performers who used these titles would be prosecuted. Houdini tried to control his challengers by installing his younger brother Dash as his main rival. Knowing that Dash worshipped him and was content to remain in second place, Houdini gave Dash the name Hardeen and arranged for him to tour Europe and the States.

Houdini's ego also made itself known in other ways. A notable incident occurred at the Houdina Company in New York, where Houdini burst in to confront the owners for using his name. A rowdy scene ensued wherein Houdini reportedly smashed office furniture. Houdini was summoned to court the next day by Francis Houdina, the owner of the company, although Houdina later dropped the charges.

Houdini was also notoriously litigious himself. He had a reputation of "raising hell" in theaters that broke contracts with him or that sued him for breaking contracts with them. At a show in Los Angeles, Houdini saw that the world heavyweight champion Jess Willard was in the crowd, and invited him to be part of the committee that sat on every stage to evaluate the authenticity of his methods. Willard refused, likely out of shyness, but when Houdini persisted, called Houdini a fake. Houdini quickly told Willard off and Willard was booed out of the theater. Houdini chastised Willard as he went, saying, "Don't forget ... I will be Harry Houdini when you are not the heavyweight champion of the world." The public supported him and he took great delight in having faced this challenge, still the great Harry Houdini.

Another challenge to the Houdini brand arrived in the form of Jacob Hyman, the young man with whom Ehrich Weiss had worked with at the clothing factory and with whom he had originally formed "the Brothers Houdini." Hyman, still practicing magic, toured New England under the name "Houdini, King of Handcuffs." He claimed that he had just as much right to the Houdini name as Harry Houdini did, as Hyman had been a part of the original duo. Houdini went after Hyman with his characteristic vigor. He sent his brother Leo to a performance of Hyman's and had him challenge Hyman to open cuffs that had been altered. Hyman could not get them open and was humiliated in front of his audience.

Houdini also battled those who threatened his fame by publicizing and selling their versions of Houdini's escape secrets. One British writer published an article announcing that escape artists concealed small keys in specially made containers that they placed in their anuses. Houdini denounced the vulgarity of this article but did not deny the claims that it contained.

Houdini also sometimes demonstrated his scorn and contempt onstage for any who copied him or who threatened to expose his secrets. When a rival magician who called himself Mysto branded himself as "the King of Handcuffs" and performed a version of Metamorphosis that involved escaping from a coffin, Houdini not only performed the same trick at his own show but then exposed how Mysto did it. Such a disclosure of another magicians' secrets is considered taboo among magicians, whose cultural norms require them to not share magic secrets with the public.

In still another battle, Houdini refused to allow Moss Empires, a large theater circuit in England and Scotland, to renew his contract, even though the original contract gave them the option to do so. After taking Houdini to court in both Scotland and England and losing, the Moss Empire sent out another performer named Hilbert, who performed escape tricks and then explained to the audience how they were done. Houdini went in disguise to one of Hilbert's shows, together with Bess and Dash. During the performance, he took off his disguise and challenged Hilbert, telling him that he had a pair of handcuffs that Hilbert couldn't open. Houdini was roughly thrown out of the theater, but had succeeded in showing the public that he wasn't afraid of Hilbert's supposed exposés.

XIV. Houdini's Last Days and Death

Read It and Know It

After reading this chapter, you will know more about

- **A bad beginning to the last tour:** Bess fell ill very early.
- **Samuel Smilovitz:** This McGill student's sketch of Houdini led him to be present during a famous moment of violence against the magician.
- **Houdini's last words:** According to Dash, the magician said, "I can't fight anymore."
- **Houdini's death:** The escape artist passed on Halloween in 1926.

During his last summer alive, that of 1926, Houdini took the months of June, July, and August "off" to rest before another season of touring with his Broadway show HOUDINI. Of course, for Houdini, "off" meant working on a book (this one about superstition), planning the founding of a magic school, and writing an article on masonry and occultism. He celebrated his final anniversary with Bess with a quiet day at the movies and one of his many love notes, as rain prevented them from taking their traditional trip to Coney Island.

Houdini's last tour began in September of 1926. It was HOUDINI but featured a new act. Houdini, locked in a bronze casket that he had made especially for the purpose, was lowered into a glass vault that was then completely filled with sand. Houdini's escape took about two minutes. The tour was set to last for five months and included appearances all over the country and in Canada. It started off on a bad note. Bess contracted ptomaine poisoning in Providence, Rhode Island, and Houdini stayed up with her all night while she battled fever and nausea. In Albany, Houdini fractured his ankle while performing the Chinese Water Torture Cell. He limped through the rest of the show. He finished his three-day tour in Albany before heading to Montreal on October 18.

The following afternoon, he gave a lecture to McGill University students. A student named Samuel Smilovitz sketched a picture of Houdini lecturing. Houdini was shown the picture at a performance that evening and he invited Smilovitz to come draw him again the following morning. Smilovitz and his friend Jacques Price arrived to Houdini's dressing room the next day to find him resting on a couch and catching up on his mail. Smilovitz began sketching while Houdini rambled at length about his various plans and recent tricks.

While Smilovitz was drawing, a young, strapping man, reportedly a first-year student at McGill by the name of Whitehead, came by to return some books that Houdini had lent him. Whitehead began talking to Houdini and asked him if it was true that Houdini could withstand any blow to his abdomen. According to Smilovitz, Houdini tried to evade the question by showing the strength of his arms and back. In truth, there is no record of Houdini ever having made a claim of resistance to abdominal blows and Smilovitz was puzzled by it. But when Whitehead asked whether he could try hitting Houdini's abdomen, Houdini, never able to decline a challenge, agreed to allow it. As Houdini went to rise to face the blows, Whitehead hit him several times with extreme force. Smilovitz and Price were shocked and cried out for him to stop. Houdini himself, winded, told Whitehead, "That will do." Although startled, Smilovitz finished his sketch, and Houdini remarked that his image looked a little tired in the drawing and that in fact he didn't feel well.

The following night, Houdini had planned a party to finish off his stint in Montreal, but had to cancel it when he was too ill to dress himself after his performance. He and Bess stuck to their schedule and boarded a train bound for Detroit that night, but Houdini experienced such terrible pain in his stomach that the group wired Detroit asking a doctor to meet them at the station. Upon arriving, the doctor quickly noticed signs of appendicitis, including a fever, but Houdini went to his hotel instead of the hospital, determined to complete his opening-night show. During a break in the show, Houdini collapsed, but was revived and insisted on continuing the show. After the show, Houdini was examined by a doctor at his hotel, who begged him to go to the hospital. After consulting with his own doctor in New York City via phone, Houdini consented and was transported to Grace Hospital.

The following day, Houdini received surgery to remove his appendix. When they opened up his body, the surgeons found his appendix grossly ruptured and enlarged and that the infection peritonitis had set in. Knowing that Houdini was at serious risk of dying from his infection, the doctors tried an experimental medicine that brought down his fever.

During the post-surgery period, Houdini remained alert and conscious, thanking all hospital staff members that performed any task for him. Houdini's brothers Nat and Hardeen and his sister Gladys came to the Detroit hospital. Bess, still recovering from her recent illness and also hospitalized, was carried to the room for brief visits. Mail poured in, and the newspapers wrote of Houdini's condition.

On Friday, October 29 Houdini received a second surgery. He did not recover from this one. Hardeen, by his bedside, later said that Houdini's last words were, "I can't fight anymore." Houdini died on Halloween, Sunday, October 31, 1926. The official cause of death was ruled peritonitis. While rumors swirled about foul play and medical malpractice, as well as the cause of death being the blows Houdini had received from Whitehead, medical evidence points to the probability that Houdini's appendix had actually ruptured some time before Whitehead punched him and that the infection had been spreading in his body for a significant period of time.

Houdini was buried in the elaborate coffin that he had commissioned for his Buried Alive stunt, in which he was to escape the locked coffin submerged in the vault filled with sand. His body was shipped from Detroit to New York City, covered in flowers, and taken to a funeral home.

Houdini was buried on November 4, 1926 in the plot where he had frequently visited his mother. His elaborate instructions for his funeral were followed, including the inclusion of his mother's letters to him in a bag as a cushion under his head in his coffin. Bess and Houdini's siblings attended the funeral, as did two thousand mourners, with two thousand more crowding the streets outside. The Society of American Magicians executed a special rite, breaking a wooden wand on the coffin.

Some of Houdini's secrets he explained during his lifetime, and some have since been discovered by others. But many went to the grave with him, leaving the world to wonder how he accomplished his marvelous feats. The people who knew, Dash and Bess, never revealed their knowledge to the public.

In Houdini's Words

After reading about Houdini and his obsession with work and fame, it should come as no surprise that he died, so to speak, in the saddle. His drive to be greater and greater is best expressed in his own words. He wrote a little of this drive in *Miracle Mongers and Their Methods*.

My professional life has been a constant record of disillusion, and many things that seem wonderful to most men are the every-day commonplaces of my business. But I have never been without some seeming marvel to pique my curiosity and challenge my investigation.

It is pleasant to think of him working until the end not because he had to, but because some "seeming marvel" had "piqued his curiosity."

XV. After Houdini's Death

Read It and Know It

After reading this chapter, you will know more about

- **Dr. Saint:** After Houdini's death, Bess possibly married her employee.
- **Communication from the dead:** Despite many attempts, Houdini never appeared at a séance to speak the agreed-upon words to Bess.
- **Bess's death:** The former performer died in 1943 of a heart attack.
- **Dash:** The magician Hardeen continued to perform in "The Houdini Show."

Bess, who upon Houdini's death announced that the world would never know what she had lost, continued to wait for a sign from Houdini. She and Houdini had made a pact that when either of them passed away, the other would await a secret, pre-agreed-upon code word to be communicated. For two years after Houdini's passing, Bess held open a $10,000 reward to any medium who could help her communicate with her husband. She waited and listened for the secret words, but found that all the mediums were full of were lies and deceit. She canceled her offer, sold 278, and moved to California. There she met Charles David Myers, who called himself Dr. Edward Saint. She hired Dr. Saint to take over her business affairs, and he devoted himself to preserving Houdini's legend. Bess and Dr. Saint were very close and it was speculated that they married, but no one knows for sure.

On Halloween night of 1936, the ten-year anniversary of Houdini's death, Dr. Saint presided over a séance on top of the Knickerbocker Hotel in Hollywood, California. Bess and over two hundred magicians were in attendance. The séance table was laid out with locked handcuffs, a gun, and a slate, for Houdini to use to impart to Bess the secret code word. After intense pleadings for Houdini to appear, nothing happened. Bess gave up. She announced that spirits did not exist and that she would not try anymore to reach Houdini. Reportedly, immediately after her declaration, a clap of thunder and a cloudburst broke the night sky.

Bess died of a heart attack in 1943, while on a train in California. Prior to her death she had announced that she would not be returning from the dead or communicating by any means with the living. She was fed up with believing such things were possible. She revealed that the secret words that Houdini and she had agreed upon to share if able to communicate as spirits were "Rosabell," the name of an old song, and the word "believe" spelled out in a special magician's code. According to her sister, who was traveling with Bess at the time of her heart attack, Bess re-converted to Catholicism during her last hours, and she was buried not next to Houdini as he had surely wished, but in a separate Catholic cemetery.

Hardeen returned to the stage after Houdini's death, performing many of his brother's famous tricks in a performance called "The Houdini Show." Hardeen lived until 1945.

■ ■

Know More About: Rosabelle

Part of the secret message from the deceased Houdini, "Rosabell, believe," comes from a song. Like so many old songs, there are multiple versions with small changes, but a common rendition is as follows:

Rosabelle, sweet Rosabelle,
I love you more than I can tell,
O'er me you cast a spell,
I love you, my Rosabelle!

The legend of Bess and Houdini claims that she sang this song in the first show she and Houdini shared very early in their careers. As such, the song had special meaning for the two.

Of course "believe" is self-explanatory. If Bess had seen that message, she surely would have.

Test Your Knowledge

I. Ehrich Weiss, the Child Who Became Houdini

1. Ehrich Weiss eventually chose the name Houdini because
    a. It was a popular term for a magician
    b. He read about Robert-Houdin, a famous magician
    c. It was unlike any other name being use at the time
    d. It was a name from the line of clothes he worked on in the factory

2. Houdini's family was
    a. Small, wealthy, and well educated
    b. Large, wealthy, but poorly educated
    c. Small, poor, and struggling
    d. Large, poor, and struggling

3. The young Houdini ran away from home because
    a. He wanted to ease some of his family's financial burden
    b. He was abused
    c. He wanted to join the circus
    d. He heard about an opportunity to become a magician

4. Jacob Hyman introduced the young Houdini to
    a. Magic tricks
    b. Gymnastics
    c. Sir Arthur Conan Doyle
    d. Drugs

II. Houdini, the Struggling Magician

1. Who were the original members of "The Brothers Houdini"?
   a. Jacob and Dash
   b. Dash and "Harry"
   c. Jacob and "Harry"
   d. Just "Harry" acting as two people

2. Houdini's popular early major escape trick was called
   a. Butterfly
   b. Chrysalis
   c. Houdini on Fire
   d. Metamorphosis

3. Who introduced Houdini and Bess?
   a. Dash
   b. Jacob
   c. Bess's mother
   d. The Rahners

4. Who was Martin Beck?
   a. Houdini's rival in love
   b. Houdini's rival in magic
   c. Houdini's stagehand
   d. Houdini's manager

III. Houdini, the King of Handcuffs

1. How was the Nude Cell Escape received in England?
    a. Terribly: Everyone was shocked
    b. Terribly: It failed to work
    c. Very well: It made a name for him
    d. Very well: It failed to work, but everyone liked seeing him naked

2. What bit of luck possibly helped Houdini win his slander lawsuit?
    a. A judge's already-open safe
    b. A sympathetic jury
    c. A jury composed mostly of magicians
    d. A snow storm

3. How did Robert-Houdin's family receive Houdini?
    a. Very well: They gave him a dinner party
    b. Very well: They let him stay at their house
    c. Poorly: They wouldn't even see him
    d. Poorly: They accosted him in public

4. Houdini performed in Russia despite what challenge?
    a. A prohibition on handcuffs
    b. A strong anti-Semitic sentiment
    c. A wrongful incarceration
    d. A prohibition on women performing, which put Bess out of commission

IV. Houdini, Back in the United States

1. What is 278?
   a. The number of times Houdini escaped from handcuffs
   b. The address of the house Houdini purchased for his family
   c. The largest number of people Houdini could draw in the U.S.
   d. The number of imitators Houdini challenged

2. For which of the following tricks did Houdini need to practice holding his breath?
   a. The Milk Can Escape and the Manacled Bridge Jump
   b. The Milk Can Escape and the Packing Case Escape
   c. The Packing Case Escape and the Manacled Bridge Jump
   d. The Packing Case Escape and the Nude Cell Escape

3. When Houdini escaped from Charles Guiteau's cell, what extra trick did he
perform?
   a. He called the jail from a different location
   b. He emerged from an underwater tunnel
   c. He swapped the other prisoners' cells
   d. He locked Bess in the cell

4. Which Boston trick almost failed and took Houdini an hour to complete?
   a. An escape from an envelope
   b. An escape from a boiler
   c. Being handcuffed to a trolley
   d. An escape from a mailbag

V. Houdini, the Aviator

1. Houdini was so seasick on his voyage to Australia that he supposedly
    a. Jumped ship and swam to shore
    b. Had to be hospitalized for his entire stay in the country
    c. Couldn't perform magic upon arriving
    d. Lost twenty-five pounds

2. How did Houdini balance performing magic and learning to fly?
    a. He didn't: he never learned to fly
    b. Poorly: He exhausted himself
    c. Well: He performed magic tricks while in the air
    d. Very well: He became the first airplane magic act to great praise

3. How did Houdini feel about boxing?
    a. He was passionate about it
    b. He was disinterested in it
    c. He was disgusted by it
    d. He never saw it

4. What was Houdini's long-term reaction to flying?
    a. He continued flying his whole life
    b. He never made it off the ground and gave up
    c. He sold his plane after a few years
    d. He became a professional pilot for the next twenty years

VI. Houdini, the Evolving Magician and Illusionist

1. Why did Houdini perform his underwater escape from a pine box in federal waters?
> a. The police prevented him from doing it in the East River of New York
> b. The police prevented him from doing it in the Charles of Boston
> c. The East River in New York was too polluted
> d. The Charles in Boston was too polluted

2. Who was Young Abe?
> a. Houdini's new assistant
> b. Dash's new stage name
> c. Bess's new stage name
> d. Houdini's eagle

3. Who was Jenny?
> a. Bess's sister
> b. Houdini's elephant
> c. Dash's wife
> d. Houdini's eagle

4. Why did Houdini begin training to stay underwater for an hour?
> a. Because he wanted to beat Charles Morritt's record
> b. Because he wanted to beat Rahman Bey's record
> c. Because he was challenged to by a fan
> d. Because Bess told him he couldn't

VII. Houdini, the Man

1. Why did Houdini eventually drop the "Harry" part of his stage name?
    a. There were too many magicians named Harry
    b. He went back to his original name
    c. Houdini sounded more regal by itself
    d. There was a lawsuit that forced him to drop it

2. How did Houdini falsify his passport?
    a. He changed his name to Dash
    b. He changed his birthplace from Hungary to America
    c. He changed his mother's name
    d. He made himself six years younger

3. Why did Houdini perform a three-hour show at Sing Sing?
    a. He was prevented from leaving by the prisoners, who loved him
    b. He was stuck underwater for much longer than he intended, about an hour and a half
    c. He wanted to beat the last magician's record
    d. He related to the prisoners, believing that he might have been one of them if circumstances had been different

4. What was Houdini's relationship with his mother like?
    a. Very controversial: she hated magic
    b. Very close: he cared for her for the rest of her life
    c. Very strained: she didn't like Bess because Bess was Catholic
    d. Very supportive: she gave Houdini money whenever he needed it

VIII. Houdini, the Writer

1. Why did Houdini resign from SAM?
   a. They told him he wasn't a good magician
   b. They tried to make him give up any tricks involving water
   c. They wanted him to be president, but he wasn't interested
   d. They wouldn't adopt his magazine, *Conjurers' Monthly*

2. Why was Houdini's book *Handcuff Secrets* controversial?
   a. Law enforcement officials worried it would help criminals
   b. He claimed the book as his own even though he didn't write it
   c. It had too many pictures of Houdini naked
   d. It described Houdini's affair

3. What does M-U-M stand for?
   a. Magic United Majesty
   b. Magicians Unmask Magic
   c. Magic Unity Might
   d. Nothing, it is a meaningless acronym

4. What was *A Magician Among the Spirits?*
   a. Houdini's movie supporting Spiritualism
   b. Houdini's book supporting Sir Arthur Conan Doyle
   c. Houdini's movie attempting to set himself up as a Spiritualist leader
   d. Houdini's book attempting to expose fraudulent mediums

IX. Houdini, the Movie Star and Producer

1. Why was Houdini interested in Hollywood?
   a. As always, he had a strong desire to stay relevant
   b. He wanted to expose the secrets of magicians on the big screen
   c. He had a bet with Dash that Hollywood would thrive
   d. He thought he could get more women there

2. What did reviewers think of Houdini the actor?
   a. They loved him
   b. They thought he was a good actor, but a bad magician
   c. They thought he was a bad actor with little range
   d. They thought what he paid them to think

3. How did Houdini's company, the FDC, do in Hollywood?
   a. Very poorly: it never got past the planning stage
   b. Very poorly: it was not financially sound
   c. Very well: it made him rich
   d. Very well: it made Dash rich

4. What was one long-term result of Houdini's Hollywood career?
   a. A lot of lawsuits
   b. A long and successful stint as an actor for Houdini
   c. A fan base in Australia
   d. The end to his marriage

X. Houdini, the Collector

1. What collection did Houdini consider his crowning achievement?
     a. His drama collection
     b. His English literature collection
     c. His stamp collection
     d. His magic literature collection

2. Houdini claimed he spent how much time working every year?
     a. Around the clock
     b. Never
     c. Five months
     d. Five weeks

3. Where did Alfred Becks work before he began working for Houdini?
     a. Yale
     b. Stanford
     c. Harvard
     d. Cornell

4. Where is Houdini's magic library today?
     a. Bess has it
     b. The Library of Congress
     c. His children have it
     d. Lost

XI. Houdini, the Crusader against Spiritualism

1. What was Sir Arthur Conan Doyle's take on Spiritualism?
   a. He was skeptical and critical
   b. He was skeptical but willing to have his mind changed
   c. He was a cautious believer
   d. He was a wholehearted believer

2. Why did Houdini's take down of Spiritualism get him in trouble with the SAM?
   a. He exposed trade secrets
   b. They all loved Spiritualism
   c. It didn't
   d. Houdini wanted all the glory for himself

3. Who was Nino Pecoraro?
   a. Houdini's mentor
   b. A medium exposed by Houdini
   c. Houdini's sidekick
   d. A rival magician

4. What was "Margery's" take on Houdini's exposure of her fraudulent practices?
   a. She hated him for it
   b. She fell in love with him after
   c. She respected him for it
   d. She did not really care

XII. Houdini, the Developer and the Patriot

1. What clubs did Houdini belong to?
   - a. The Masons
   - b. The SAM
   - c. The London Magicians Club
   - d. All of these

2. Why was Houdini not drafted in World War I?
   - a. He was too old
   - b. They didn't trust him
   - c. He was not a U.S. citizen
   - d. He never signed up

3. Which of the following was part Houdini's effort to aid the war?
   - a. He stopped performing magic
   - b. He helped the army enlist more magicians
   - c. He entertained the troops
   - d. He donated money to the troops

4. What dangerous trick did Keller prevent Houdini from performing?
   - a. The Upside Down
   - b. Staying underwater for an hour
   - c. Trying to free himself while riding a bull
   - d. Catching a bullet from a gun

XIII. Houdini, the Proud

1. What word best describes the perception of Houdini amongst his peers?
    a. Humble
    b. Boring
    c. Educated
    d. Egotistical

2. What was Houdini's reaction to imitators?
    a. Tolerant
    b. Aggressive
    c. Passive
    d. Disinterested

3. When heavyweight champion Jess Willard refused to participate in his act, Houdini
    a. Tried to convince him but gave up
    b. Did not try to convince him
    c. Pushed Willard until Willard punched him
    d. Pushed Willard until they fought and Willard was booed out of the theater

4. When Jacob Hyman claimed he had a right to the Houdini name
    a. Houdini had him humiliated in front of an audience
    b. Houdini bribed him to stop
    c. Houdini conceded
    d. Houdini rekindled their friendship and brought Hyman into his act

XIV. Houdini's Last Days and Death

1. What two events marked a bad beginning to the final tour of HOUDINI?
> a. Bess broke her ankle and Houdini fractured his
> b. Bess caught pneumonia then gave it to Houdini
> c. Houdini fell ill and Bess broke her ankle
> d. Bess contracted ptomaine poisoning and Houdini fractured his ankle

2. What was Houdini's response to Whitehead's aggressive attack?
> a. He said, "That will do"
> b. He fled
> c. He punched his attacker
> d. He shot his attacker

3. Despite early signs of appendicitis
> a. Houdini performed a five-hour show
> b. Houdini went to his hotel instead of a hospital
> c. Houdini went home
> d. Houdini performed the Milk Can Escape

4. One of Houdini's instructions for his funeral was
> a. To be buried with both his and Bess's wedding rings
> b. To be buried upside down
> c. To be buried with his mother's letters
> d. To be buried in a Catholic plot so he could be with Bess

XV. After Houdini's Death

1. Bess responded to her husband's death initially
      a. By trying to forget about him
      b. By remarrying
      c. By trying communicate with him
      d. By never leaving the house

2. Were Bess and Dr. Saint married?
      a. Yes
      b. No
      c. For a little while
      d. It is uncertain

3. Why was Bess buried in a Catholic cemetery?
      a. She had re-converted to Catholicism
      b. Her mother forced her to be
      c. She wasn't
      d. Houdini had wished it

4. After his brother's death, Dash
      a. Gave up magic
      b. Continued to perform
      c. Died after only a month
      d. Married Bess

Test Your Knowledge Answer Key

I. Ehrich Weiss, the Child Who Became Houdini

1. b
2. d
3. a
4. a

II. Houdini, the Struggling Magician

1. c
2. d
3. a
4. d

III. Houdini, the King of Handcuffs

1. c
2. a
3. c
4. b

IV. Houdini, Back in the United States

1. b
2. a
3. c
4. b

V. Houdini, the Aviator

1. d
2. b
3. a
4. c

VI. Houdini, the Evolving Magician and Illusionist

1. a
2. d
3. b
4. b

VII. Houdini, the Man

1. c
2. b
3. d
4. b

VIII. Houdini, the Writer

1. d
2. a
3. c
4. d

IX. Houdini, the Movie Star and Producer

1. a
2. c
3. b
4. a

X. Houdini, the Collector

1. d
2. c
3. c

4. b

XI. Houdini, the Crusader against Spiritualism

1. d
2. a
3. b
4. c

XII. Houdini, the Developer and the Patriot

1. d
2. a
3. c
4. d

XIII. Houdini, the Proud

1. d
2. b
3. d
4. a

XIV. Houdini's Last Days and Death

1. d
2. a
3. b
4. c

XV. After Houdini's Death

1. c
2. d
3. a

4. b

Made in the USA
San Bernardino, CA
10 June 2016